# HERBLOCK
# THROUGH THE
# LOOKING GLASS

# HERBLOCK THROUGH THE LOOKING GLASS

*Herbert Block*

*W · W · Norton & Company*

*New York   London*

The text of this book is composed in Times Roman, with display type set in Bulmer.
Composition and manufacturing by The Haddon Craftsmen Inc.
Book design by Nancy Dale Muldoon

FIRST EDITION    SECOND PRINTING

Library of Congress Cataloging in Publication Data

Block, Herbert
Herblock through the looking glass.

1. United States—Politics and government—
1981-    —Caricatures and cartoons. 2. Reagan,
Ronald—Cartoons, satire, etc. 3. American wit and
humor, Pictorial. I. Title.
E876.B57  1984    973.927    84–16697

ISBN 0-393-01929-2

W. W. Norton & Company, Inc., 500 Fifth Avenue, New York, N.Y. 10110
W. W. Norton & Company Ltd., 37 Great Russell Street, London WC1B 3NU
2 3 4 5 6 7 8 9 0

ONCE MORE
TO
JEAN RICKARD,
WHO HAS MADE
ANOTHER BOOK
POSSIBLE

# AMONG FRIENDS

I belong to the three-chimpanzees school of writing. Those are the theoretical chimps who, if they beat away at three theoretical typewriters for enough eons, would produce words in proper sequence to make a book or a play. I save a few eons, thanks to friends who look over various drafts, marking what to keep and what to run through the machine a few times more.

Jean Rickard edits everything from the roughest beginnings, consults with publisher, works on the entire book layout, frequently on a round-the-clock schedule, and generally does everything that can be done for a book. Ed Rickard goes to any length to see that it gets out on time.

Again, on this book, two people went over every version of every chapter: Bob Asher, office neighbor and longtime valued colleague; and Robin Meszoly, a national editor who not only knows just the right words for the right places, but also the right facts to go with them. Both have also gone over cartoon sketches day after day. Their generosity with their time and their editing were better than a freightload of bananas and rubber tires for the chimps.

Thanks again to two others who took time from their own writing to go through every chapter: Doree Lovell, who has now helped edit four of my books—all of them improved by her expertise and her inner ear for phrases; and Haynes Johnson, whose unerring judgment sorts out book chapters as well as cartoon sketches.

Jane Asher and Bob even called in galley corrections from phone booths while on an outdoors vacation.

Donna Canzano enthusiastically helped with all phases of preparation and tracked down statistics, transcripts and background material—as did researchers Carla Liverman and Bridget Roeber. Olwen Price and Lynn Elmehdaoui made extra efforts to meet publishing schedules.

Several colleagues with particular knowledge on special subjects checked over one or more chapters, often while fighting their own deadlines: Karen DeYoung, Howard Kurtz, Dale Russakoff, David Hoffman, Fred Hiatt, Peter Milius and Howard Simons.

There are more—Jodie Allen, Pat Shakow, J. W. Anderson, Mary Thornton, Dick Homan, Mike Causey, Terri Shaw, Murrey Marder, Joseph L. Rauh Jr., Michael Barone and Jim Dickenson. And—Fred Barbash, Joanne Omang, John M. Berry and Molly Sinclair.

To give proper mention and appreciation to each one would require a whole nother chapter. All I can say is Thanks!

And as the chimps would add: A whole bunch!

H.B.

# CONTENTS

**THROUGH THE LOOKING GLASS**
*June 3, 1984*

# LOOKING-GLASS LAND

Anyone who has appeared before a TV camera has later heard acquaintances exclaim, "I saw you on television!" Once when I was on a TV program a friend of mine sat down with a friend of hers to watch. *Her* friend (who has met me dozens of times) sat with glazed expression until I was introduced, then rose, wide-eyed, from her chair, pointed to the TV set and cried, "It's him! It's HIM!" It must have been like a kind of religious experience—the miracle of telecommunications, as they say. She believed because she saw—on the TV set. Such is the impact of this medium.

Russell Baker wrote a column about a man who discovered that a person didn't really exist until he was on TV. After the man was killed in an accident, his picture appeared on the screen, and thus he finally became alive after he was dead.

Television critic Tom Shales has wryly observed that incidents in real life can sometimes move us almost as much as the commercials that feature little heart-tugging relationships to sell products.

Before our eyes there pass—with blurring rapidity—news shots of actual events, the brief scenarios of commercials and the characters

©1983 HERBLOCK

**"THE BUTLER DID IT"**
*May 19, 1983*

in movie stories. The "docudramas" go a step beyond. They show actors portraying real-life people in a homogenized part-fact, part-fiction film product that has the effect of putting history, soap opera and the viewer's brains in a blender.

Household items are sometimes displayed in stores with a sign "As shown on television." This certifies that they actually exist and that you don't have to depend on the mere fact that you can pick them up, see them, feel them and use them. Broadcast commercials have long told us of detergents that make laundry cleaner than clean and whiter than white. TV tends to make itself more real than reality. Its impact on our lives is enormous. Its effect on politics is staggering.

When 1984 finally arrived, endless words were poured out about how the actual year compared with the situations in George Orwell's book—a novel, incidentally, which was named almost at random and which was not intended as prophecy. With great relief, writers noted that in our country the paraphernalia of government torture and the omnipresence of Big Brother on two-way television screens were not in evidence.

But the number 1984 and the two-way screen were irrelevant. The significant political fact was the power of the regular one-way screen showing not a scowling Big Brother but a genial president, elected under a democratic system, with the ability to shape perceptions through the looking-glass of the TV set.

In the early days of the medium somebody put out the word that the all-seeing eye of TV could detect true character and could tell truth from falsehood. That observation was itself a first-class falsehood. On television you can't always tell whether the person who comes across as real is the one with or without makeup—or which person took lessons in how to appear natural.

On the tube, what you see is what you get—an image projected on a screen. But some images are more attractive than others.

Since the days of Richard Nixon's "Checkers speech" in 1952, and the televised appearances of John F. Kennedy, observers have been aware of the growing influence of TV on politics. There has always been some Hollywood hype in Washington such as staged presentations. Political "photo opportunities" include ethnic meals and various styles of headgear.

**"ON YOUR HEADS, FOLKS—I HAVE A MANDATE TO DO THINGS DIFFERENTLY"**

*March 29, 1981*

*January 22, 1984*

**GREAT COMMUNICATOR**

*March 19, 1982*

**"THIS WILL BE FOLLOWED LATER BY CORRECTIONS AND OFFICIAL EXPLANATIONS OF WHAT HE MEANT TO SAY"**

*February 20, 1983*

But Ronald Reagan brought us, after only a few years of made-for-TV movies, our first made-for-TV president. Washington became Hollywood East. And if the medium wasn't actually the message, it was the means through which almost any message could be conveyed in a manner as convincing and warm as commercials for telephones or hot dogs.

Mr. Reagan was the ideal person to make this possible. His experience embraced not only a couple of decades of politics, but careers as movie actor, radio sportscaster, broadcaster of political messages and host for sponsored TV programs.

These skills, combined with a president's power to dominate the news and to get broadcast time, created what amounted to a new political equation—Reagan vs. reality—the taking of the public through the looking glass.

In the spate of articles about 1984, some commentators noted that we did have an increase in a kind of newspeak. Tax increases had become "revenue enhancers," a gas tax was a " user fee," MX missiles were "peacekeepers," and the description of American troops in Lebanon as "peacekeeping forces" continued long after they had ceased to keep the peace.

It is just as well that the peacekeeping forces were not provided with peacekeeper missiles. Lt. Robert Goodman, who was flying in a bomber that was shot down over Syrian-held territory, was described by President Reagan as a man who had been on a mission of peace.

In one case at least, the creative euphemism didn't work. After U.S. forces moved into Grenada, Reagan berated the press for using the term "invasion" instead of "rescue mission." Some news programs then re-ran the tape of Reagan's earlier reference to our "invasion." Through the magic of videotape, memory survived.

Reagan is said to have learned valuable lessons in communication from listening to the speeches of Franklin Roosevelt. But there were striking differences—even apart from their policies in the White House. There's an oft-told story about Roosevelt. When he became president, he was troubled to find that he would have to follow a fiscal policy different from one he had suggested in a campaign

"DAMN MEDIA! YOU SHOULD KNOW
BETTER THAN TO REPORT ALL THE
DOPEY THINGS HE SAYS"
*January 28, 1983*

"WHAT I MEANT WAS: SCORING IS
ONLY A GOAL"
*November 10, 1981*

"AND THEN A BIG DRAGON CAME
AND BUST THE JAR AND ATE ALL
THE COOKIES"
*October 9, 1983*

"SORRY, KID, BUT THAT'S SHOW BIZ"
*November 18, 1981*

speech at Pittsburgh. Adviser Sam Rosenman dryly cracked: "Deny you were ever in Pittsburgh." The point here is that Roosevelt was *concerned* about the discrepancy.

Not so with Reagan. After promising a balanced budget and after having spent most of his political life denouncing deficits and unbalanced budgets as the root of all evils, including inflation, he ran up the biggest deficits in history. He did so without even going through the motions of offering Congress a balanced budget. He simply continued to denounce deficits and to blame them on Congress and preceding presidents. He also offered a constitutional amendment to require future administrations to balance the budget.

As an added twist he described his opponents as being latecomers to the virtues of holding down deficits. None of this had any connection with his own actions or previous promises. But there was no need for a memory hole. Reagan used the broadcast-listener like a cassette tape on which a new recording automatically erases previous recordings.

When the U.S. Information Agency, under Reagan's appointee Charles Z. Wick, was criticized for putting out propaganda at the expense of factual reporting, Reagan had a ready reply. He recalled his early days as a sports announcer, when he recreated accounts of baseball games as they came over the ticker, filling in with his own local color and some imagined plays. He explained that this was an example of how truth could be bent with no harmful effects. But he did not differentiate between a man giving a sports rendition on an Iowa radio station in the 1930s and an agency of the United States government broadcasting news to the world in the 1980s. Nor did he seem to note any difference between Iowa sports announcer Reagan and President of the United States Reagan.

In a non-sports radio broadcast in February 1984, President Reagan said that Lebanese support for the government of President Amin Gemayel and for his army were increasing—this at a time when both were crumbling. And we were also making "great progress" while leaving Beirut.

Reagan differed from his predecessors not simply because he had been an actor and an announcer but because to him there was appar-

©1981 HERBLOCK

**"LEAVE THE FACADES—IT'LL BE JUST LIKE HOLLYWOOD"**

*December 1, 1981*

ently no distinction between delivering statements as president and delivering lines as an actor—*it didn't matter* whether the words were factual. It only mattered that they were presented well and that they sounded good to the audience. If an anecdote worked effectively in a speech, he would use it again, even if it turned out to have no basis in fact.

An example of fiction and reality turning themselves inside out occurred in an incident that Reagan described with some emotion in several speeches. And he eventually included it in a presidential address to winners of the Congressional Medal of Honor. He told about a B-17 bomber in World War II being hit as it was returning from Occupied Europe to its base in England, and about a ball-turret gunner being wounded and unable to parachute out with the rest of the crew. As the pilot was about to jump, he heard the wounded and frightened gunner, went to him and said, "Never mind, son. We'll ride it down together." Reagan concluded with the words, "Congressional Medal of Honor, posthumously awarded."

Lars-Erik Nelson, of the *New York Daily News,* felt that the story did not ring right despite Reagan's claim to have actually read the medal citation. Nelson wrote that each of the 434 Medals of Honor awarded during World War II was accompanied by a citation that described the precise circumstances and reasons for the award. Reagan's anecdote was not among them.

But a World War II veteran helped straighten out the story. As he told Nelson, the incident did not take place aboard an Army Air Force bomber over the English Channel with a wounded turret gunner. It took place in a Navy torpedo bomber over the Pacific with a wounded radio operator in a three-man crew. The gunner bailed out—but the pilot did go down with the wounded radio man, saying, "We'll take this ride together." One other thing: It didn't actually happen in World War II. It happened in a 1944 war film, "Wing and a Prayer."

In a classic through-the-looking-glass anecdote, Reagan, claiming that busing for school desegregation "has failed in its purpose," told the story of Linda Brown. Her name became famous in 1954 when the Supreme Court ruled against segregation in *Brown v. Board of Education.* Because of segregation, Linda had been bused past a

*December 10, 1981*

"GREAT SCOTT! A HERD OF WILD DONKEYS!"

*March 10, 1982*

"AT NIGHT THEY COME DOWN FROM THERE AND MAKE ME DO THESE THINGS"

*October 29, 1982*

"HOW ABOUT TEDDY-ROOSEVELT LAND—CONSERVATION AND ANTI-TRUST POLICIES?"

*August 7, 1981*

white school near her home to a black school on the other side of town.

Later, when she became Mrs. Linda Brown Smith, she had a daughter of her own. As Reagan told it, Linda Brown Smith is now "opposed to busing in her own community because, she said, now her daughter is bused miles past the school near her home."

Now for the facts: (1) Linda Brown Smith's daughter attended a public school two blocks from her home; (2) Topeka, where her daughter went to school, did not employ busing for racial balance; and (3) Mrs. Smith said she would not be opposed to busing for desegregation if it were necessary.

White House staff members were unable to document the Reagan story, but said they stood by it.

As Alice said about Looking-Glass house, "The books are something like our books, only the words go the wrong way."

Another anecdotal story was related by Lou Cannon, Reagan biographer and White House correspondent, in a 1984 newspaper column:

> When Israeli Prime Minister Yitzhak Shamir visited the White House last Nov. 29, he was impressed by a previously undisclosed remembrance of President Reagan about the Nazi extermination of Jews during World War II.
>
> Repeating it to his Israeli Cabinet five days later, Shamir said Reagan had told him that he had served as a photographer in a U.S. Army unit assigned to film Nazi death camps.

Later:

> On Feb. 15, famed Nazi-hunter Simon Wiesenthal met with Reagan in the White House and heard a similar story. Wiesenthal told Washington Post reporter Joanne Omang that he and Reagan had held "a very nice meeting," during which the president related "some of his personal remarks from the end of the war."
>
> Rabbi Marvin Hier, dean of the Simon Wiesenthal Center in Los Angeles, also was present. He told Omang that Reagan said he was "a member of the Signal Corps taking pictures of the camps" and that he had saved a copy of the film and shown it a year later to a person who thought the reports were exaggerated.
>
> "He said he was shocked that there would be a need to do that only one year after the war," Hier said.

*September 28, 1983*

"NOW, AS YOU CAN SEE ON THIS CHART . . . "

*March 27, 1983*

"CHIEF, NOW YOU COULD ELIMINATE THE INCOME TAX AND SOCIAL SECURITY TAXES"

*November 14, 1982*

*February 19, 1982*

Actually, Reagan, who made training films in Hollywood during the war, had not served abroad. After Cannon's column appeared, Reagan denied that he had ever told anyone he had served outside the country.

Following a December 1983 press conference in which Reagan gave a long account of recent events in the Middle East, columnist Robert Kaiser annotated the Reagan version of history, pointing out inaccuracies in every paragraph. An example:

Describing the invasion of Lebanon by Israel and its attempt to drive out the Palestine Liberation Organization in 1982, Reagan said: "In the meantime, during all of this, the Lebanese asked the Syrians —asked them to come in and help preserve order in Lebanon. . . . "

Syrian troops actually came into Lebanon, not "during all of this" in 1982, but six years earlier in 1976.

Kaiser concluded his article with the observation that "generally the news media now treat Reagan's slips as par for the course" and "the White House staff no longer bothers to correct his mistakes."

Reagan's misstatements were not limited to mangled history or to Hollywood triumphs over reality. Nor were they simple slips. Reagan frequently tossed off statistics having little or no relation to facts. He made statements that blacks were better off before the Great Society programs of President Johnson.

In March 1984, he said that in "the early '60s, we had fewer people living below the poverty line than we had in the later '60s after the great war on poverty got under way."

U.S. Census Bureau figures showed otherwise: the number of Americans living below the poverty line dropped from 39.9 million in 1960 to only 24.1 million (12.1 percent) in 1969. Additionally, the number below poverty level rose during the Reagan years. So the Reagan numbers didn't jibe with official government figures—but they *sounded* authentic.

Similarly, Reagan statements about great progress of women and blacks in his administration also turned out to have no visible means of support.

Reagan said that toward the end of the Carter administration unemployment was going up. Actually it was going down.

**"MUCH BETTER THAT WAY"**

*March 7, 1984*

**SPECIAL ASSISTANT FOR VOODOO AFFAIRS**

*May 4, 1982*

**"ARE YOU SURE WE NEVER SENT CONGRESS A BALANCED BUDGET? I'VE ALWAYS TALKED ABOUT BALANCED BUDGETS IN ALL MY SPEECHES"**

*July 30, 1982*

**"I WANT YOU TO LEVEL WITH ME, SON—NO REAGANTALK"**

*June 17, 1983*

While many Reagan claims were completely inaccurate, some were mere exaggerations. For example, in a 1983 speech he said that 600,000 new businesses had started up the year before. This was just a little more than double the actual number—which was under 300,000.

David Stockman, Reagan's director of the Office of Management and Budget (OMB), tried to correct some pumped-up figures on supposed administration savings when he realized that they were not reflected in the budget. Stockman found that his deputy had sent the White House a suggestion for a Reagan radio speech saying the administration had recaptured $12.5 billion last year through improved debt collection. As reported by David Hoffman and Pete Earley in *The Washington Post* in May 1984:

> Of this $12.5 billion, Stockman discovered upon investigation, $5 billion was simply for crop loans that farmers had repaid in the regular course of business when prices rose and they redeemed grain they had left with the federal government in storage.
>
> Stockman sent a memo to Richard G. Darman, deputy White House chief of staff, indicating that the $12.5 billion claim was exaggerated, an OMB official said.
>
> But the president used the figure on the radio anyway on March 3 . . . "we boosted collections by $12.5 billion last year."

Before the presidential numbers that didn't come out right, there were the campaign promises that didn't add up. In 1980, presidential candidate John Anderson said of candidate Reagan's promise to increase arms spending, cut taxes and balance the budget that "It's very simple—you do it with mirrors." Reagan did better than use mirrors. He took the public *through* them to Looking-Glass Land in which things looked the opposite of what they were.

With breathtaking political *chutzpah* he cut federal aid to education and blamed the schools and teachers for not doing a better job. And then, after bestowing his favors on corporations and wealthy individuals, he cried out about "special interests" when his opponents sought to help the poor, the unemployed and the disabled.

He beat the drums for organized vocal prayer in the public schools while asserting that this was to protect "religious freedom."

"I'M ALWAYS TRUE TO YOU, DARLING, IN MY FASHION"

*July 25, 1982*

Could a commander-in-chief accuse his opponents of wanting to "bug out" of Lebanon at the very time he was himself preparing to withdraw the troops? Why not? In Looking-Glass Land, where we had a new morality and a new reality, nothing was impossible. As Ronald Reagan's popularity soared in the polls, many voters apparently felt about him—in the words of the old song, "You're My Everything"—*You're my only dream, my only real reality / You're my idea of a perfect personality.*

In 1982, political scientist James David Barber wrote that "Ronald Reagan is the first modern president whose contempt for the facts is treated as a charming idiosyncrasy." And he reminded readers that Thomas Jefferson said, "The whole of government is the art of being honest."

The sheer volume of the Reagan misstatements made it impossible to correct them all. Only occasionally could commentators alert readers or viewers to some of them (and usually be accused of nit-picking or *lèse majesté*) as still more misrepresentations continued to pour out.

By February 1984, conflicting White House stories about the "redeployment" (withdrawal) of Marines from Lebanon got a little too thick even for loyal supporters in Congress. Trent Lott (R-Miss.), the House minority whip, felt the administration had been so misleading that he exploded, "You people are not in touch with reality." It could have been that even the real reality of televised speeches was wearing thin.

A month later, in March 1984, the Democratic majority leader in Congress spoke up with words that were plain and direct. Said Jim Wright of Texas:

> Mr. Speaker, it pains me to have to correct inaccuracies uttered by the President of the United States about meetings which I attended and which he did not. . . . He says at one point [about bipartisan meetings on the deficit] that we offered no ideas or suggestions at all. That is a lie. It is untrue. I personally offered as many as 20 different suggestions. All of them were summarily rejected. . . .
>
> He said, "We had great difficulty getting them to even meet," talking about the Democrats. That is a lie. That is not true. That

is a falsehood. They had no difficulty getting us to meet. We met every time we were invited. . . .

It is just that plain. It is a lie. They had no difficulty getting us to meet. On two occasions I suggested dates. . . .

He said on one occasion that we, and I am quoting, "just simply walked away on one issue and refused to talk." That, my colleagues, is a lie. I hate to say that of the President of the United States. It is the same kind of a lie that he told when he said that the House was dragging its feet on an anticrime bill after we, in a session just previously, had passed an omnibus crime bill and he had vetoed it.

Maybe it is not an intentional lie. If it is not, it is amnesia.

The Capitol dome did not fall in, nobody was struck by lightning, and the members across the aisle did not faint dead away. There might have been a few raised eyebrows and even a few raised eyelids. TV viewers and newspaper readers who caught his words seemed to survive very well.

Somebody might have said, as Alice did when she rubbed her eyes at the end of her strange adventures, "You woke me out of oh! such a nice dream! And you've been along with me . . . all through the Looking-Glass world."

Well, some of it anyhow.

# STAYING ALIVE

The ever-increasing numbers of health and fitness manuals are enough to provide constant exercise running to book and record shops. Some of the body-building drills make the Laocoön serpent wrestlers look like smug slobs. And for us softies, the routines are enough to strain the mind before they can ever get to the muscles. There are also diet regimens that are less punishing to the outer body but that leave the stomach crying, "What the hell is going on up there?"

Fortunately, a great deal of progress toward longer and healthier lives has been made by simple exercises of free speech, by people walking—not running—to meetings of fellow citizens, and by selective hand movements in voting booths.

Such activities have helped to reduce the hazards of chemical warfare, toxic exhausts, and dangerous pesticides, and to improve the environment for living beings. But, like most exercises, they need to be practiced regularly.

An example of what can be done by a few people and a few groups can be seen in public reaction to drunk-driving fatalities that used to

**"TODAY'S AUTO FATALITIES: THREE PEOPLE DIED IN ACCIDENTS, AND FOUR MORE WERE KILLED BY DRUNK DRIVERS"**
*November 24, 1982*

**ONE MORE FOR THE ROAD—26,000 MORE FOR THE YEAR**
*December 30, 1981*

**AMERICAN CAR BOMB**
*December 16, 1983*

**"MAN, I'VE GOT TO HAVE WHEELS"**
*July 6, 1982*

be accepted as more-or-less natural deaths, or "accidents." It's estimated that more than 20,000 motor-vehicle deaths a year are "alcohol-related."

The idea of "one for the road" used to be as common as "fill 'er up" instructions were at gas stations. And law enforcement generally was lax, probably because many of those who did the enforcing could visualize themselves in the same situation.

Candy Lightner, whose child was killed by a drunk driver in May 1980, was soon joined by others in forming an organization called Mothers against Drunk Driving (MADD). This group and others have succeeded in changing laws and attitudes about driving-while-intoxicated cases.

Anyone who still thought living it up behind the wheel of a car was amusing must have been brought up sharply by a 1982 case in Virginia where a man driving at high speed ran a red light and swerved into an oncoming traffic lane. In a head-on collision, two teen-age girls were killed, as well as a passenger in the wrong-lane car. The driver was charged not with "driving while intoxicated" or

**"BUT I NEED MY DRIVER'S LICENSE TO GET AROUND"**

*January 10, 1982*

**"HITTING THAT CHILD WITH YOUR CAR MUST HAVE REALLY JOLTED YOU. KEEP YOUR DRIVER'S LICENSE AND GET YOURSELF A COUPLE MORE DRINKS"**

*March 24, 1981*

**"BUT IT WAS AN ACCIDENT—AFTER A FEW DRINKS, IT COULD HAPPEN TO ANYBODY"**

*March 14, 1982*

**"A FEW DRINKS CERTAINLY WON'T AFFECT A GOOD DRIVER LIKE YOU"**

*July 3, 1983*

**TOBACCO ROAD**

*March 31, 1982*

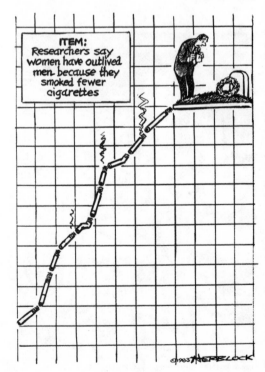

**"YOU'VE COME A LONG WAY, BABY"**

*August 11, 1983*

even "involuntary manslaughter" but with second-degree murder. In several other states, similar charges had been pressed and had also resulted in convictions.

The alcohol industry, which does not need this kind of trouble, warns against mixing drinking and driving. On holidays it also runs ads urging those who have been celebrating to stay away from the wheel.

But the tobacco industry—whose products don't produce instant injury and whose effects are less visible than automobile treadmarks —maintains there is no proof that smoking is dangerous. It continues to run ads suggesting that tobacco products contribute to fun and good living. The ads are often set against a background of God's

"NO, WE DON'T HAVE A NO-SMOKING SECTION—WITH
THE KIND OF FOOD WE SERVE HERE, WE DIDN'T THINK
TASTE MADE ANY DIFFERENCE"

*May 29, 1984*

**AMERICAN ROULETTE**
*December 18, 1980*

**"I DUNNO ABOUT FOREIGN AID—IN SOME OF THOSE COUNTRIES, LIFE IS CHEAP"**
*April 10, 1981*

**"YOU CAN DO A FAVOR FOR ME— RUB OUT ANY GUN CONTROL LEGISLATION"**
*August 7, 1980*

**"YOU MEAN THAT'S JUST AN EXPRESSION?"**
*June 11, 1981*

great outdoors, where the vigorous cigarette-smoking cowboy may later need all the oxygen he can get. But there is something to be said for that cowboy out there. Whatever he's doing to himself, he's not fouling the air for some guy at the next desk or for restaurant patrons who would like to taste their food.

Sen. Jesse Helms (R-N.C.), who has been kind of a smokesman for this lobby, has compared tobacco to alcohol and suggests that people who regard its effects as dangerous should frankly advocate its prohibition.

But the government does not subsidize the alcohol industry as it does the tobacco industry. Most non-users of tobacco are not prohibitionists or people who feel about their fellow workers that where there's smoking there must be firing.

The old saying about freedom of speech—that the other person's rights stop where my nose begins—applies literally to smoking. More and more people are recognizing that there is a right not to be an involuntary or second-hand smoker.

While many adults have given up cigarettes, much of the smoking lately has been done by youngsters—particularly girls. The tobacco industry says that—perish the thought—it does not encourage kids to smoke and wishes they would wait until they are adults to make this choice. But the industry's agents who pass out free cigarette packages where young people congregate don't always distinguish between adults and children.

Cigarette advertising is often connected with sporting events largely attended by young people. Sponsorship of these events suggests a connection between smoking and healthy, active sports, like tennis. The cigarette companies don't sponsor surgical wards, which could carry signs saying, "You've come a lung way, baby."

The tobacco industry, which figures that non-smoking is hazardous to its wealth, has spent millions of dollars setting up smokescreens about smoking-restriction referendums. Their heavily financed efforts were unsuccessful in San Francisco. In 1983 that city voted to limit smoking in those work places and public areas where it would affect non-smokers who felt "Yes, I mind."

But at the federal level the tobacco influence seemed to remain

*September 11, 1980*

**"YOU SHOULD BUY A COUPLE TO
PROTECT YOURSELVES AGAINST
THESE OTHER SATISFIED
CUSTOMERS"**

*March 8, 1981*

**"EVERYBODY DOWN ON THE FLOOR
AND DO EXACTLY WHAT I TELL YOU"**
*March 25, 1982*

**NEWS OF THE DAY, EVERY DAY**
*December 10, 1980*

34

habit-forming. In the June 1984 bill to increase tax revenues, Congress inhaled deeply and cut in half the federal tax on cigarettes.

The tobacco industry maintains that there is no causal relationship between smoking and lung cancer—or emphysema or heart disease. To this industry, all the charts and statistics and operations are just funny coincidences. There is no "smoking gun"—only a long chain of smoking cigarettes.

The handgun lobby, on the other hand, is not even concerned about smoking guns. It recognizes that there are thousands of smoking guns connected with fatalities. But it argues that there is nothing wrong with the easy access of handguns because it is "people who kill people." But people are not particularly designed to kill people —handguns are. Pistol shooting at non-human targets is a minor

**"GOSH, THAT TYLENOL POISONING STORY HAS REALLY BEEN SCARY"**

*October 20, 1982*

35

**FOUR OF THE LAST EIGHT**
*March 31, 1981*

*May 14, 1981*

**ACCESSORY**
*December 9, 1980*

**"BACK TO THE ROUTINE NEWS"**
*May 15, 1981*

sport, and people who feel at home on those ranges can keep their pistols there. But handguns are made for the primary purpose of being fired at other people. And the people who kill with them are often children. They find guns lying around the house and sometimes have to use both their little hands to pull the trigger.

The inaccurately titled National *Rifle* Association (NRA), the gun manufacturers and the criminals who all profit from the widest possible sale of handguns consistently resist efforts to control them. These groups do not limit their intensive and expensive lobbying against ordinances that would restrict the availability of handguns. The NRA has also lobbied for the repeal of those modest federal restrictions on some lethal weapons that were enacted after the murder of Robert F. Kennedy.

The NRA showed its concern for gun sales as opposed to human life and crime-fighting when it even opposed restrictions on the sale of special cartridges designed to pierce otherwise bullet-proof vests.

"WHAT'S HAPPENING—ARE PEOPLE
FINDING THEIR MINDS? IS
EVERYONE GOING SANE?"
*March 5, 1982*

"WHEW—THANK GOODNESS YOU'RE
NOT INJURED IN A VITAL PLACE"
*October 5, 1983*

**"WE'RE GOING TO GIVE IT MORE STUDY"**
*February 21, 1984*

**"HOW ABOUT HAVING IT GIFT-WRAPPED?"**
*December 14, 1980*

**"WE HAVE NO EVIDENCE OF ILL EFFECTS—WE HAVE NO EVIDENCE OF ILL EFFECTS—THIS IS A RECORDING—"**
*September 28, 1980*

**THE THIRD CORNER**
*November 16, 1982*

These vests are most often worn by policemen and by public figures who might be targets for assassins.

On July 18, 1984, a man entered a fast-food restaurant in San Ysidro, Calif., and randomly killed 21 men, women and children. He carried an Uzi semi-automatic rifle, a 9 mm Browning automatic pistol and a Winchester 12-gauge shotgun. These guns are legal for over-the-counter sale in most of the country. Police said he broke no laws in carrying them into the restaurant. As a requirement for purchasing a firearm legally, a buyer must swear that he is not mentally incompetent. The most common requirement, of course, is that the gun purchaser have the money to buy it.

Many of us were shocked when John Hinckley, who had tried to assassinate President Reagan, was found not guilty by reason of insanity. We shouldn't have been. When there is little regulation of the sale or registration of the millions upon millions of handguns floating around the country, why should we be shocked at a little individual insanity connected with a gun?

The town of Morton Grove, Ill., decided in 1983 that it had had enough and put a flat ban on all handguns. And the gun lobby screamed as if it had been—well—shot. The lobby tried and failed to have this kind of sanity ruled illegal.

In response to the Morton Grove action, the ruling council of some little town got itself a brief mention by decreeing that every householder *must* possess a gun. I don't know the follow-up to that. Before this ruling could have been declared unconstitutional, maybe they all knocked each other off.

Most of us could probably use some keep-fit routines to improve our bodies; but it's something just to keep those bodies vertical and breathing. Okay, class, a little exercise of common sense—a turning down of the thumbs on those businesses and organizations that put a fast buck ahead of longer lives . . . that's it . . . one and two . . . and three . . . thumbs straight down and let's hear a little growling . . . that's it . . . fine! . . .  ■

"HELLO, BIPARTISAN TOWING COMPANY? IT'S ME AGAIN"

*January 27, 1984*

# THE MONEY TREE

We all realize that technology has altered our lives. Computers can be used by everyone, including children. They figure in shopping, learning and transactions of all kinds. But such things are obvious and superficial. The real computer revolution runs deeper. It has changed everything since the days of Adam and Eve. Computers have eliminated guilt, responsibility and human error.

When you get a bill that is six hundred dollars too high, does the bill-sender apologize? Does he explain that an employee made a mistake? No. He says the computer did it.

Computers make all the mistakes now—on bills, tax notices and statements of all kinds. The fault, Dear Brutus, is not in our stars but in our computers. To err is computer, to forgive human.

Although the new freedom from error started with businesses, computers are now for homes and for schoolwork too. No longer will the dog eat the homework, or some mysterious malefactor steal a book report before it can be handed in. The computer will have swallowed it—gulped it right down its memory blank. The school-child can even explain that the homework couldn't be done at all. "Sorry, teacher—computer down."

**"SIR, EVEN SOME OF THE
PASSENGERS UP IN FIRST-CLASS ARE
GETTING WORRIED"**
*January 22, 1982*

**"I BRING THE FLOWERS AND HE
BRINGS THE RAIN"**
*February 2, 1982*

**THE NEWEST FEDERALISM**
*January 30, 1983*

**"IT'S INSTEAD OF THAT BALANCED
BUDGET WE PROMISED"**
*August 2, 1983*

At any rate we are now used to computer error. So when I heard in 1984 that I, and the rest of us U.S. taxpayers were in debt to the tune of a trillion-and-a-half dollars, I figured the machines were up to their new tricks again.

But I talked to a financial writer who had talked to somebody at the White House who said it was so. Including interest, we do owe more than a trillion-and-a-half dollars, with the meter still ticking and well on its way to $2 trillion. The White House explained that the debt was no longer a big worry and besides it was caused by previous administrations.

I still didn't understand how that debt could have nearly doubled in four years, especially when Reagan said we would have a balanced budget in 1983.

Well, it was a real relief to know that the people running the government were good old-fashioned folks who didn't blame everything on computers. They blamed the previous tenants, the politicians across the aisle, "the Fed" or some other outfit down the street. But not to worry about the deeper-than-ever deficit. We are over our heads but we are standing tall in the hole.

I remember only a few years ago when these same people told us that the federal budget was just like a family budget—you could only spend as much as you took in. How many families are $200 billion in debt for the year, or a trillion-and-a-half dollars total—I mean even with his-and-hers credit cards?

Obviously things have changed some. Actually, they've changed a lot since I took an economics class in school. At that time they said basic needs were food, clothing and shelter—and they didn't mean tax shelter. That will just give you an idea. Before economics I had a little math, in which they said two plus two equals four. This is another notion that went out on Inauguration Day, Jan. 20, 1981.

Economics has never been simple, but Reaganomics has made it even more complicated. To help us understand what's been going on since January 1981, let us start with a brief glossary.

| Supply-side economics: | On the side of people who are well supplied. As in *money side of the street.* |

43

| | |
|---|---|
| **Special interests:** | Poor people, members of labor unions, handicapped people, teachers, dependent mothers and their rotten kids. |
| **Out years:** | (not to be confused with election off years): Years that have not come in yet. Future deficits—out of sight, out of mind, out of pocket. |
| **Deficit:** | (*obs.* or before 1981): Worst thing in the world; a fate worse than debt; total disaster; cause of inflation and incurable diseases; invariably fatal. *Current usage:* inherited illness, not so dangerous as thought. See *budget*. |
| **Budget:** | Something that should have been balanced before and should be balanced in the future, but not right now. |
| **Depression:** | Any economic dip before 1981, as in *Carter Depression*. |
| **Recession:** | Economic slump, formerly due to government. Since 1981, a natural cyclical event; an Act of God. |
| **Recovery:** | Emergence from recession; caused by wise policies and strong leadership. As in *recovery policies leading world out of recession*. |
| **Defense:** | Magic word; any amount of money for anything not related to improving the lot of people. Defense funds: necessary to survival. *Syn:* essential; sacred. Defense Department: formerly U.S. Treasury and U.S. mint. |
| **Feldstein:** | Former economic advisor. Oddball. White House *derog. pronunciation:* Feld-steen or Feld-stine. |
| **Interest rates:** | (1) Rising—caused by Federal Reserve or someone else. (2) Falling—result of White House policy. |

| | |
|---|---|
| **Welfare:** | Handouts to freeloaders and other undeserving. |
| **Waste, fraud and abuse:** | See *Welfare*. |
| **Needy:** | See *Waste, fraud and abuse*. |
| **Truly needy:** | Other recipients of handouts. |
| **Truly indeedy needy:** | Otherwise decent people who have gone bad. |
| **Deserving poor:** | See *Truly needy*. |
| **Safety net:** | A collection of holes. |
| **Whistle blower:** | A troublemaker; one who interferes with defense spending. A bad apple. |
| **Federal Reserve:** | An independent board often responsible for anything that goes wrong with finances or the economy. |

We can now proceed to a brief summary of events since the arrival of Reaganomics.

The Reagan program, offered in the 1980 campaign, was to cut taxes, increase military spending and balance the budget. As usual there were doubters who thought this wouldn't work.

They were right. It didn't.

Taxes—particularly for the wealthy and for corporations—were greatly reduced. Military spending, already increased under Carter, now went up sharply. And the budget, which was to have been balanced in 1983, shot upward.

With lower taxes and bigger spending, the deficit broke all records. By 1984, David Stockman, director of the Office of Management and Budget (OMB) looked ahead and stared at $200 billion deficits as far as the eye could see.

This was despite the best efforts of the OMB to put the best face on administration policies. In 1981, when the projections fed into the computers did not produce figures that jibed with administration forecasts, new projections were fed in. People don't cook the books any more. They cook the computers.

**"WE'VE GOT TO STOP WRINGING OUR HANDS"**

*August 15, 1982*

**"THEY WERE LEFT UNDER A CABBAGE LEAF BY PREVIOUS PRESIDENTS"**

*February 2, 1983*

**"WE THINK IT'S RELATIVELY SHALLOW"**

*November 8, 1981*

**"GOSH, SON, WE'RE ALL TOGETHER AGAIN"**

*June 4, 1982*

**"OH, THOSE THINGS ARE THE FAULT OF CONGRESS OR THE PAST SEVERAL ADMINISTRATIONS OR SOMETHING"**
*January 19, 1982*

**"IT'S STILL TRICKLING UP"**
*April 8, 1982*

**"IT SAYS HERE THAT THINGS HAVE TURNED THE CORNER"**
*March 6, 1983*

**"I THINK WE CAN DEFINITELY SAY THAT THINGS ARE LOOKING UP"**
*July 7, 1982*

**"WHAT I SAID WAS—IT'S SUCH A
BEAUTIFUL HORSE IT SHOULD BE
ENTERED IN THE NEXT DERBY"**

*November 13, 1981*

**"WE'RE SURE SOME MORE
OPERATIONS WILL MAKE US FEEL
BETTER"**

*February 3, 1982*

**"WHERE DID YOU GET THESE CRAZY
IDEAS ABOUT THE DANGER OF
DEFICITS?"**

*December 11, 1983*

**"WE'RE IN THE TROUGH OF THIS
RECESSION"**

*May 2, 1982*

The administration condemned previous administrations for what it called a policy of "tax and spend." But it didn't explain how there would be improvement in a policy of "tax less and spend more."

In December 1981, *The Atlantic Monthly* published an article by William Greider titled *The Education of David Stockman.* In this article, based on a series of interviews, Stockman talked frankly about his problems and the administration. He spoke about its policy of aiding the wealthy in the hope that money would eventually trickle down to the lower levels—an old Republican policy associated with Herbert Hoover. Stockman said, "It's kind of hard to sell 'trickle down,' so the supply side formula was the only way to get a tax policy that was really 'trickle down.' "

The same kind of euphemism could be applied to the Reagan Recession, which brought both unemployment and business failures to the highest levels since the Great Depression of the 30s. The recession might have been called a "course adjustment," or an "anti-inflation" policy, on which we needed to "stay the course." But the old expression for what happened was "putting the country through the wringer." That's what we went through before we were "on the mend."

Economists sometimes tend to run on, or to get pretty esoteric. But Isabel Sawhill, of the Urban Institute, gave a brief explanation of what happened in 1981. She said, "Tight monetary policy endorsed by this administration led to a recession. The business downturn, along with some fortuitous softening of oil and food prices, produced a substantial drop in the rate of inflation."

Nothing lasts indefinitely, not even the worst of times. In the days when people had no idea what caused plagues, the plagues eventually ran their course.

Consumer items don't last indefinitely either, and in recent years they seem to wear out sooner.

Eventually the car or the washing machine has to be replaced. So people begin to buy, even though their incomes are down and prices stay up. On car prices, for example, auto companies and dealers acted as if the law of supply and demand had been repealed. Confidence in recovery undoubtedly helped to bring about better times.

"AND WE KNOW YOU'LL VOLUNTEER
TO PAY MORE FOR CARS YOU DON'T
LIKE AS MUCH"

*March 19, 1981*

"AS A LAST RESORT, WHAT IF WE
TRIED COMING RIGHT OUT AND
TELLING THE CUSTOMER OUR BEST
PRICE?"

*November 1, 1982*

"WE DON'T KNOW MUCH ABOUT
RECOVERY—WE'RE HERE BECAUSE
OUR 1972 CAR DIED"

*July 14, 1983*

"SOME GUY WITH A NUTTY IDEA
ABOUT SELLING MORE CARS AT
LOWER PRICES"

*February 29, 1984*

But at any rate consumer buying is generally credited with providing the economic boost that came in 1983.

There was a certain irony in the administration blaming Congress for our national budget problems. Congress was to blame to the extent that in 1981 it gave Reagan the kind of tax bill he wanted and also voted for his increased arms spending programs. What was unnecessary cruelty to docile creatures was Reagan's accusing them of being "budget-busters" when they later made some modest changes in his domestic spending cuts.

A popular British comedy duo gave their television program a title based on both their names: "The Two Ronnies." In Washington, we also had Two Ronnies—two presidents, but not for the price of one, and not even for the price of two or a dozen presidents. One Ronnie kept saying, "There's only one major cause of our economic problem: government spending more than it takes in and sending you the bill." Meanwhile, the other Ronnie was adding to the national debt by almost as much as all previous presidents combined.

Sen. Ernest F. Hollings (D-S.C.) is not one to suffer fools gladly or to take political trickery and abuse lightly.

When President Reagan claimed that Congress could offer no alternative to his budget, Hollings promptly answered the challenge. He proposed a budget plan that included a temporary spending "freeze." His plan was widely praised, but not by the Reagan administration, which did not really want an alternative budget. Hollings also had something to say about the politics of the Reagan policies: "He intentionally created a deficit so large that we Democrats will never have enough money to build the sort of government programs we want."

Hollings said that Reagan came to the White House "to preside as the referee in bankruptcy over the dismantling of the American government." And he pointed out that from 1950 to 1970 the whole cumulative government deficit was $74.7 billion—compared to the $457 billion Reagan added to the federal debt in his first 32 months in office.

©1984 *HERBLOCK*

**"YOU FIRST, SON"**
*January 3, 1984*

Readers who find numbers numbing can take heart. Here is one more quote from *The Atlantic Monthly* article on David Stockman:

> The budget politics of 1981, which produced such clear and dramatic rhetoric from both sides, was, in fact, based upon a bewildering set of numbers that confused even those, like Stockman who produced them.
> "None of us really understands what's going on with all these numbers," Stockman confessed at one point. . . .

What could easily be understood—especially by those who were the victims of the numbers—were their effects: cuts in programs for the poor, the hungry and the disabled. While running up skyrocketing arms costs and vastly increasing the national debt, Reagan prided himself on these cuts.

One of the most illuminating and significant facts about the entire Reagan administration budget policy appeared in a *New York Times* story by Robert Pear on Feb. 15, 1984. Here is the lead on that story (the boldface type is mine):

> **President Reagan's proposed budget for the fiscal year 1985 shows that the increase in the interest payments on the federal debt since he took office exceeds all the savings his administration has achieved in health, education, welfare and social service programs.**

Pear's story goes on to give the figures: Under the Reagan 1981 budget the government would pay $47.4 billion more in interest on the national debt than the amount spent for the same purpose in 1981. The Congressional Budget Office estimates that since January 1981 legislative changes have reduced federal spending on social welfare programs $39.6 billion below what it otherwise would have been in 1985.

That's where the money goes—and after all those "savings" on programs for people. That's also the answer to those who think, to paraphrase Gertrude Stein, that a deficit is a deficit is a deficit.

Previous modest deficits provided for adequate real defense and

*November 23, 1982*

**"WE'VE TOLD YOU BEFORE, FELDSTEIN—YOU'RE NOT HELPING WITH THE TOURIST TRADE"**

*May 10, 1984*

**"IT'S NOT AS IF WE WANTED YOU TO LEAVE THE TEAM, FELDSTEIN"**

*December 2, 1983*

*August 14, 1981*

for domestic programs and still left balanced budgets within reach. The out-of-control deficit does not.

With the *interest* on the debt running between $115 billion and $150 billion a year, consider how much would be needed in taxes or spending cuts just to keep even. Consider also how much new borrowing is needed at new interest rates to pay the old interest on the old borrowing. As the Red Queen said to Alice, "Faster! Faster! . . . Here it takes all the running *you* can do to keep in the same place. . . ."

There was another *Alice in Wonderland* quality about the administration fiscal 1985 budget. Almost as soon as it came out, presidential economic advisor Martin Feldstein and budget director David Stockman let it be known that the budget no longer reflected official policy. The administration marched a budget up the Hill and marched it down again. The budget non-budget appeared and disappeared like a Cheshire Cat.

Immediately after that came the Economic Report of the President, prepared by the President's Council of Economic Advisers; and this was brushed aside by Secretary of the Treasury Donald Regan, who said we should forget it.

"Oh my fur and whiskers!"—right down the rabbit hole.

For the third year in a row, the budget buck was passed to Congress by an administration that billed itself as providing "leadership."

When unemployment was shooting up in 1982, Reagan pooh-poohed the fuss about "some fellow in South Succotash someplace" who has "just been laid off." But thanks to Reaganomics, well-to-do fellows in Palm Beach, Palm Springs or wherever were laid back—enjoying more government benefits than ever.

The wealthy and the big special interest groups went untouched by the sharp blade of the budget ax.

Corporations paid less taxes than ever. Capital gains taxes dropped. There were generous incentives to companies that hardly needed more incentives. The oil companies—which hardly needed a few billion in extra incentives—could be grateful to Reagan. So could the dairy lobby, which could continue milking the taxpayers. The

**"MAGIC OF THE MARKETPLACE"**
*May 13, 1982*

*July 31, 1983*

**"I DON'T THINK I CAN KEEP UP WITH YOU"**
*November 15, 1983*

**"IT'S THE WORST-CASE SCENARIO—OUR BUDGET IS UNDER ATTACK"**
*February 3, 1983*

tobacco lobby continued getting support. Trade restrictions benefiting the sugar lobby were costly to consumers—and so were the "voluntary" Japanese restrictions on automobile exports and the restrictions on textile imports.

With inflation easing, the administration lost no opportunity to talk about how it had saved us from what it called the "inflation tax." But this same administration was not vocal about the extra billions paid by taxpayers and consumers in special benefits or "corporate-welfare taxes" and "trade-restriction taxes."

The administration explained that its tax benefits were really fair by pointing out that the rich pay more taxes than the poor. And in all fairness to the administration, that's right, up to a point—if you ain't got nothin', you don't pay nothin'. But with the Reagan tax changes, the lower incomes did pay relatively more than the higher incomes.

An example of a little extra welfare for the wealthy was cited in a *Washington Post* editorial in June 1984, which began, "Of course you've heard the horror story about the welfare recipients who drive late-model Cadillacs. . . ."

It then explains that this is true—of wealthy recipients.

> Ever since the enactment of the 1981 tax bill, people who buy luxury cars for primarily business use have been able to get the Treasury to pick up a major part of the tab. Thanks to a 6 percent investment tax credit and the ability to write off a car in three years, the buyer of a Rolls, for example, might realize over $65,000 in tax benefits in three years. "With these kinds of figures," advertises one car dealer, "a luxury isn't a luxury. It's a wise investment."
>
> That "investment" looks even better when you consider that a high-priced import will hardly degenerate into a pile of scrap metal in three years, as the tax law now supposes. Even the average car loses only about half its value over four years, and a top-of-the line Mercedes, for example, may lose as little as 10 percent. The lucky purchaser, having realized all his tax benefits in three years, can then look forward to years of private use.

Such welfare for the wealthy provides a little frosting on the cake for those already counting their benefits. Some of those "wise invest-

**"HE'S HAD US ON THE MEND FOR A LONG TIME NOW"**

*February 4, 1983*

**"LOOKING FOR SACRED COWS?"**

*February 11, 1981*

**"OF COURSE IT'S FREE ENTERPRISE—THESE FELLOWS WERE ENTERPRISING ENOUGH TO GET THINGS FOR FREE"**

*December 23, 1983*

**"TOO BAD THOSE PEOPLE HAVE SUCH A LEAKY BOAT"**

*June 23, 1981*

ment" private luxury cars have undoubtedly driven past the private sector soup lines that the administration views with suspicion.

The public sector also provides opportunities for savings that would hardly leave anyone destitute.

Government pay and pensions are a big item in the federal budget. Some early retirements cost the government the services of useful military personnel. Early retirement plus generous pensions for government personnel, who then do a little consulting work, enable many to make more money after they leave the government than they did while employed by it.

Anyone who thinks that civilian government employees work at a sacrifice might be interested in a March 1983 letter to the editor in *The Washington Post* from Karen W. Ferguson, director of the Pension Rights Center—a public interest group. It was written in response to a *Washington Post* editorial calling for adequate government pensions to supplement Social Security benefits for future government employees who would be brought under that system. Wrote Ferguson:

> If "a supplementary pension comparable to a good private-sector plan" [Social Security Roadblock," editorial, March 17] is all that new federal workers can expect in exchange for Social Security, the government employees' unions have reason to be concerned.
>
> The very best private-sector plans—those of the largest and most profitable companies—typically require 10 years of work before an employee earns the right to a pension; the current civil service plan requires only five years. . . .
>
> Unlike the Civil Service Retirement System, pension benefits provided by good private sector pension plans are rarely indexed for inflation. At best, they provide occasional, and inadequate adjustments.
>
> Private plans also provide far less protection to widows and widowers. The government employees' unions are more than justified in demanding to know what their pension plan will look like. At the very least they are entitled to a firm commitment from Congress that the new plan will be better than a comparable "good private-sector plan."

Government employees, who also enjoy automatic pay increases and more job security than most, seldom agree publicly that they

**"WELL, THEY WORK ON CONGRESS, AND THAT'S THE MAIN THING"**

*August 4, 1982*

**"THEY FIGHT OVER THE SIZE OF THEIR CUTS TOO"**

*February 20, 1981*

**"ROLL IT OUT AGAIN—THIS BUNCH WILL PROBABLY BUY IT"**

*June 5, 1981*

**"EVERY ONCE IN A WHILE WE'RE BOUND TO BE ON TARGET"**

*February 25, 1982*

have a better deal than the private sector generally offers. Nevertheless they have fought to keep the system they have.

But the Big Daddy of government Big Spenders is the Defense Department. When the Pentagon shakes the money tree, billions come cascading down like dry leaves.

Any secretary of defense may have a hard time keeping costs under control. But to a secretary of defense in an administration that is eager to pay out for anything labeled "defense," the sky is the limit.

Why build one new-type bomber like the Stealth when you can build two or more new ones—including the B-1 and upgraded B-52s? The fact that the new Stealth will replace the other new planes is no reason to turn down an opportunity to make some extra aircraft—especially when the costs run high enough to justify bigger and bigger arms budgets.

Then there are the interservice rivalries that result in duplications of planes and weapons of many kinds. Secretary of Defense Caspar Weinberger was like a doting parent of three or four children. Such a parent finds it easier to see that each gets everything any of the others has.

That means we are not only in an arms race with the Russians—we are in an arms race with ourselves.

It's not only costly—it doesn't provide us with the best defense.

The administration likes to wrap the Defense Department in the flag and suggests there is something unpatriotic about criticizing its spending programs. But who are the better patriots—the officials who purchase untested and malfunctioning weapons and waste billions of dollars in contract ripoffs, or those who believe that the money spent on defense ought to buy us the best defense we can get?

In defending Reagan administration arms programs questioned by Congress, Secretary Weinberger said that giving up some of those programs would mean losses of jobs. This threat may have been, in fact, a statement that let the cat out of the bag. While the administration deplored New Deal type "make-work" programs, it had more expensive ones of its own—arms programs to keep factories humming.

**"WE CALL HIM 'CAP, THE LADLE' "**
*March 6, 1981*

**"IS THERE ANY KIND OF GAS THAT WILL *GIVE* PEOPLE NERVE?"**
*November 9, 1983*

**"IF THE RUSSIANS START ANYTHING, WE'LL SHOOT MONEY AT THEM"**
*November 28, 1980*

**TODAY'S MAKE-WORK PROJECTS**
*October 22, 1982*

The threats to business and jobs were effective with Congress. And there's probably truth in the story that in planning some arms programs—notably the B-1 bomber—Pentagon contractors managed to have parts produced in as many congressional districts as possible.

There was very little Congress didn't approve except new nerve gas weapons to replace old ones. The multiplicity of nuclear weapons gave Congress pause about the MX missile, but not enough to prevent the spending of many billions to go forward with it.

The Pentagon resisted calls by congressmen for competitive bidding, for proper testing of weapons and for warranties on Pentagon purchases.

Sen. Mark Andrews (R-N.D.) wanted to know why it was that he could get a warranty for his tractor, but the Army couldn't get one for its tanks.

A united front of Pentagon officials and arms manufacturers opposed such proposals for better performance of defense materials. It would slow up the purchasing.

Rep. Jim Courter (R-N.J.) sponsored a bill to increase competitive bidding in arms programs and services. When he sent copies of the bill to the Defense Department, asking for comments, the responses were that his letter was being forwarded somewhere else in the Pentagon and that a reply was being prepared. Finally he was told that it was forwarded to the Office of Management and Budget. The OMB said that "no such letter had been received for review."

The path of the whistle blower has never been smooth, and was made no easier under the Reagan administration despite high-flown talk about rooting out waste, fraud and abuse.

Vernon A. Guidry, Jr., writing in *The Baltimore Sun*, recalled that shortly after taking office, Reagan said, "Federal employees or private citizens who wish to report incidents of illegal or wasteful activities are not only encouraged to do so, but will be guaranteed confidentiality and protected against reprisals . . . they must be assured that when they 'blow the whistle,' they will be protected and their information properly investigated."

But, Guidry wrote, "Despite official rhetoric praising the government whistle blower, the formal machinery for punishing federal

**"OH-OH—ANOTHER WHISTLEBLOWER WHO CALLED ATTENTION TO EXCESSIVE COSTS"**
*November 18, 1983*

**"YOU SEE, ACTUAL WEAPON-TESTING WOULD SLOW UP THE SPENDING PROGRAMS"**
*July 5, 1983*

**"WHATEVER IT'LL DO ANYWHERE ELSE, IT SURE FLATTENS EVERYTHING AROUND HERE"**
*January 7, 1982*

**"NEXT YEAR, BABY—"**
*December 9, 1983*

officials who try to silence whistle blowers or conduct reprisals against them has never produced so much as a wrist slap." He wrote about George Spanton, a resident auditor at a Pratt & Whitney facility in Florida, who had complained internally about excessive labor costs, travel and lavish entertainment for Pentagon officials used in computing costs to the government. Mr. Spanton got a transfer order, which he said was "in reprisal for his lawful actions as an auditor and federal employee."

The most famous whistle blower was A. Ernest Fitzgerald, who in 1969 was fired by President Nixon after he told Congress about cost overruns on the C-5A cargo plane. He fought his case and in 1982 a federal court ordered him reinstated in a Pentagon position on financial management. But in 1984, under the Reagan administration, the Air Force was so reluctant to let him give official testimony to Congress that a Senate subcommittee subpoenaed him.

Fitzgerald testified that "I have the responsibility in the Air Force, theoretically, to do should-cost studies" but "I'm just not allowed to do it." He said a "blue curtain" had been drawn around him, because, he believed, of Air Force embarrassment about significant overcharging on most weapons systems. And he had "never seen a major weapons system that on first examination could not be cut at least 30%." He cited Hughes Aircraft Co. overcharges for Maverick missiles and said that similar procedures would have resulted in a TV set costing $100,000.

Sen. Charles E. Grassley (R-Iowa) said it was "a scandalous situation" that Fitzgerald could not get the information he needed. To illustrate the administration's attitude on whistle blowers and cost-watchers, Secretary Weinberger said he thought Grassley was just trying to get good headlines.

Obviously, cost-watchers had to be kept down—at any cost.

In one of his candid statements, budget director David Stockman called the Defense Department a "swamp of waste."

But an administration that had trumpeted its war against "waste, fraud and abuse" in penny-ante welfare cheating could not seem to ferret out such things in a Defense Department where waste, fraud and abuse got the red carpet treatment.

"I NEVER UNDERSTOOD WHAT THAT RECESSION WAS THAT PEOPLE TALKED ABOUT"

*December 28, 1983*

"WE'RE GOING TO GET THERE IN STYLE"

*January 24, 1982*

*July 27, 1983*

"YOU'LL BE HEARING ALL KINDS OF HORROR STORIES ABOUT MY PROGRAM"

*February 12, 1982*

What finally forced the administration to recognize this obvious state of affairs were some easy-to-understand examples. An administration that had itself specialized in horror stories (often fictional) to attack "people programs" realized the impact of for-real horror stories.

An Air Force man who found a plastic tip missing on the foot of a stool tried to get a plastic tip through channels. As the plastic-tip project became entangled in requisitions and red tape, he decided to follow it all the way and was staggered by what he found.

The Pentagon paid $1,118 for a plastic cap worth 17¢.

Other examples began pouring forth like skeletons tumbling out of a closet.

A socket wrench worth $1.49 cost the Pentagon $466. An Allen wrench is available at retail hardware stores for 12¢. The special wholesale price paid by the Pentagon: $9,606 each.

And this was only a partial list.

In December 1983, Sen. William Roth (R-Del.), a persistent watchdog, put up a Christmas tree decorated with some Pentagon purchases. These included a small bolt that cost the Pentagon $1,075.

A $17 hammer: $435.

A 13¢ nut: $2,043.

A $3 flat washer: $387.

A 9¢ screw: $37.

A 2½¢ antenna motor pin: $7,417.

The cost of all the items on the Christmas tree to individual retail purchasers: about $100. The cost to the Pentagon: about $100,000.

As Sen. Roth observed, the Pentagon played Santa Claus all year.

In an old story, a suit salesman tells a customer that he loses money on every suit he sells. When asked how he can do it, he replies, "It's the volume." The Pentagon could afford to lose a thousand dollars on every dollar item because of the volume of taxpayers' money it could lay its hands on.

Just when the administration was hoping the articles about $1,000 wrenches were over, another series of horror stories came out in July 1984. These concerned Pentagon buying-and-selling-and-buying-back practices—the selling of brand new spare parts at junk prices and repurchasing of replacements at high prices. For example—

**SURVIVAL OF THE FATTEST**
*February 16, 1982*

**BIGGEST BARRELED GUN IN THE ARSENAL**
*March 2, 1983*

**"I BELIEVE I DO SEE A LITTLE SOMETHING—BUT, AFTER ALL, I'VE ONLY BEEN ON THIS JOB FOR TWO AND A HALF YEARS"**
*July 20, 1983*

**"WE COULDN'T TRIM ANYTHING MORE WITHOUT CUTTING INTO FAT"**
*January 13, 1983*

In 1983, the Air Force disposed of $700 million in spare parts, many still in good condition. The Army sold for $65 an $8,000 machine still in its unopened shipping carton. Some junk-sale items were still in the original cartons when salvage dealers sold them *back* to the Defense Department.

When those first exorbitantly expensive nuts and bolts began dropping out of the mighty Pentagon spending machine, President Reagan met the situation in a radio speech. He expressed outrage about the outrage over these items and claimed that it was the administration's own investigators who had uncovered these abuses. Hah! Independent inspectors had been forced on a reluctant Reagan administration that had wanted all investigations to be in-house projects.

Moreover, network television programs, operating with their own staffs, had given millions of viewers examples of jiggered figures by Navy contractors and other defense suppliers. When Reagan and Weinberger found waste, fraud and abuse in the Pentagon, it was like someone living at the base of Mount Everest suddenly claiming to have discovered that mountain—after spending all its time examining molehills.

The real discovery has been made by people who have found that official talk about economy has no relation to the economy itself.

The government computers that register astronomical debt may look as if they've gone haywire, but they haven't.

It's the officials who need to be checked out.　　■

**"THEY CALL IT AN
ACROSS-THE-BOARD POLICY"**
*February 12, 1981*

**"I HOPE IT'S NOTHING SERIOUS"**
*October 20, 1981*

**"PRETTY GOOD STUNT—NOW LET'S
TRY IT AGAIN WITHOUT THE SAFETY
NET"**
*November 1, 1981*

**"AND IN NO TIME AT ALL, IT CAN
CLIMB TO AN ALTITUDE OF . . ."**
*November 11, 1981*

**"WATCH ME HIT THAT DAMN JAPANESE CAR"**

*July 20, 1980*

**"IT'S CALLED HARA-KIRI-KABOB"**

*March 26, 1981*

*October 23, 1981*

**"WITH ALL RESPECT TO YOU, CAP'N, SIR"**

*February 24, 1982*

**"IT'S A FIFTY-FIFTY DEAL—YOU TAKE OVER WELFARE AND WE MAKE SURE PEOPLE HAVE TO GO ON IT"**

*February 23, 1982*

**"SORRY . . . THAT JOB HAS BEEN FILLED . . . THANK YOU . . . SORRY . . . THAT JOB HAS—"**

*May 8, 1983*

*April 22, 1982*

**"I WONDER IF YOU JACKASSES—I MEAN NOBLE FRIENDS—"**

*August 18, 1982*

**"WE ALREADY HAVE A JOBS PROGRAM"**

*December 14, 1982*

**"IF WE KEEP ON WITH THE ARMS RACE, AFTER A WHILE THE RUSSIAN ECONOMY WILL COLLAPSE"**

*December 8, 1982*

**"WELL, I ALREADY HAVE LAST YEAR'S EDITION—AND A MAGAZINE"**

*February 9, 1982*

**"GOODNESS KNOWS I LASHED MYSELF TO THE MAST"**

*January 19, 1983*

*March 20, 1983*

**LAST LINE OF DEFENSE**
*April 4, 1982*

**"IT MAKES USE OF THE HOLES IN
THE GROUND WE ALREADY HAVE"**
*July 12, 1983*

**"YOU CAN'T MOVE THAT ONE—IT'S
'CAP' WEINBERGER"**
*December 29, 1982*

"THIS IS CAPTAIN REAGAN SPEAKING, AND I'M STILL WAITING
FOR YOU PEOPLE BACK THERE TO FLY THIS PLANE PROPERLY"
*March 4, 1984*

*April 22, 1984*

*January 29, 1984*

**CUT**

*March 27, 1984*

**"AND BY THE TIME WE FINISH
PAYING FOR IT, WE MIGHT THINK OF
SOME REASON FOR HAVING IT"**

*May 18, 1983*

**"HURRY—I THINK HE'S COMING BACK AGAIN"**

*April 3, 1984*

**"EGAD—I AM MORTALLY WOUNDED"**

*September 9, 1981*

**"OH, OH—THERE IT GOES AGAIN"**

*October 9, 1980*

**"BROTHER, CAN YOU SPARE A HUNDRED BILLION OR SO TOWARD THE INTEREST ON THE LAST TRILLION OR TWO?"**

*April 15, 1984*

**"HOW THE HELL DO YOU EXPECT TO BEAT THE RUSSIANS WHEN YOU
KEEP FORGETTING THE SECRET HANDSHAKE, GENERAL?"**

*October 23, 1983*

# IN THE DARK OF
# THE MOON

There has always been lots of appeal in the idea of being in on something secret—the private, hidden, exclusive, inside secret.

KIDS! Send in three box tops and you can have your very own decoder ring!

*NOW, you can buy this ordinary looking little cabinet, which has a hiding place that only YOU know about!*

This shack is our very own boys' club, members only, no girls allowed!

*If the members of this mystic organization, meeting in cloistered conclave, decide you are worthy to be admitted, you may enter the candle-lit inner sanctum and learn the secret rituals.*

And if you are successful enough in a business organization, who knows, you might get a key to the executive washroom.

Nobody has ever advertised: *GROWNUPS! RUN FOR OFFICE! If you get enough votes, you can have your very own government and your very own secrets!* But too often people who do get enough votes feel that along with the private limousine, the government also becomes their private personal domain, with all kinds of secrets and

March 24, 1982

knowledge—too good to let the public in on. The Press, whose stories are anything but secret, becomes the enemy at the gates.

Every president has worried about leaks. Generally the leaks are not of vital information, but are annoying disclosures of differences within an administration or premature releases of information scheduled for announcement at a more politically opportune time. Usually the principal leakers are government officials themselves—often the very ones who complain about *unauthorized* leaks.

John F. Kennedy said that the ship of state was the only ship that leaked from the top. When Lyndon Johnson was president, an accurate news story about his intention to remove a high official from public office sufficiently irritated him that he reversed field and announced he was keeping the official. Richard Nixon, interviewed on television in 1984, said, "I was paranoic, or almost a basket case with regard to secrecy. . . ."

But probably no president brought to the White House a fear of public information and a mania for secrecy to match Ronald Reagan's. Within his first three months in office he issued an executive order making it easier to withhold public documents under the rubber-stamp phrase of "national security." Where President Nixon had used "plumbers" to plug leaks, Reagan tried to turn off the tap of information at the source. The methods used were legal, if not honestly presented.

Over a period of 30 years, presidents of both parties tried to cut back on the overclassification of documents and made more papers public. Nixon was reported to have been surprised that more than 100 million papers from World War II remained classified.

But President Reagan reversed the trend toward more public information. In the name of national security, he increased the number of classified papers. He nullified President Carter's order that called for *review* of classified records after 20 years. Instead of following a standard that secrecy labels be used only where necessary, the Reagan order required that everything possible be stamped secret—and that papers be kept classified for longer periods of time.

The order even provided for *re*classification of previously unclassified and public documents.

The administration also sought to curb information available

**"SHAME ON YOU, RUNNING AROUND LIKE THAT—QUICK, PUT THIS OVER YOUR HEAD"**

*August 27, 1982*

**"JERRY FORD WAS A PIKER. REAGAN GIVES SPECIAL CITATIONS WITH HIS PARDONS"**

*April 17, 1981*

**"THOSE LITTLE BARRIERS ARE JUST TO STOP MAD BOMBERS—THIS IS TO PROTECT AGAINST PUBLIC INFORMATION"**

*February 5, 1984*

**"IT DIDN'T SEEM RIGHT TO KEEP HIM COOPED UP"**

*May 8, 1980*

through the Freedom of Information Act. What it could not do through changes in the act itself, it did largely by delaying tactics, by withholding more "classified" material and by charging high fees for copies of documents.

But that was not all. There was also wider protection for officials whose work might impinge on public rights—a policy made clear within the first three months of the Reagan administration.

In April 1981, two former high FBI officials who had been convicted for their parts in illegal break-ins on innocent citizens won not only President Reagan's pardon but also his praise.

Later that year the administration drafted a plan to give the CIA latitude to engage in domestic surveillance. The proposed order provided for "special activities [covert actions] . . . and such other intelligence activities as the president may direct from time to time." The plan was opposed by the entire Senate Intelligence Committee, including its chairman, Barry Goldwater.

Reagan also lost no opportunities to express greatest confidence in the military and to overlook errors of U.S. military leaders.

No president outside of a totalitarian country or a government of rotating coups seemed so eager to ingratiate himself to the military, to police agencies and to secret operatives. Reagan even had a penchant for giving military salutes.

In October 1981, the administration proposed a "Freedom of Information Improvements Act"—the "improvements" being a greater withholding of records.

The following year, CIA Director and Reagan crony William J. Casey said in a speech to the American Legion that he questioned "very seriously whether a secret intelligence agency and the Freedom of Information Act can co-exist for very long." And he added, "The willingness of foreign intelligence services to share information . . . will continue to dwindle *unless we get rid of the Freedom of Information Act.*" The italics are mine, as is the naked-Casey cartoon on the subject. Later, Casey asserted in a public letter that his position had been "distorted"; he said he felt that "the benefit to the public from F.O.I.A. releases is marginal." But, goodness, he "never advocated the total repeal of the act." That's what he wrote.

A measure that served the dual purpose of pleasing the CIA

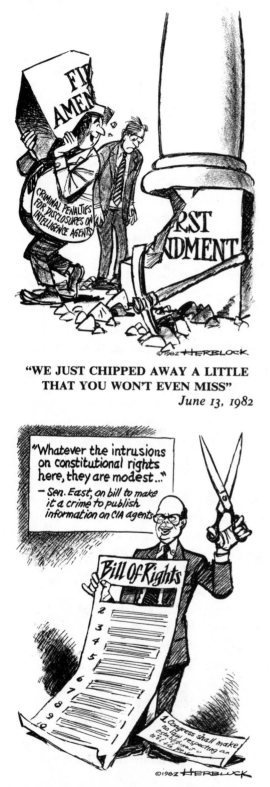

**"WE JUST CHIPPED AWAY A LITTLE THAT YOU WON'T EVEN MISS"**

*June 13, 1982*

**"THE *OLD* CIA WOULD HAVE KEPT THE RUSSIANS OUT OF AFGHANISTAN—THE SAME AS IT KEPT THEM OUT OF CZECHOSLOVAKIA, HUNGARY, CUBA . . ."**

*February 3, 1980*

**"IT STILL LEAVES AMENDMENTS 2 THROUGH 10"**

*March 3, 1982*

**"WE HAD TO DO IT—HE PULLED A PEN ON US"**

*September 5, 1980*

leadership and taking a swipe at press freedom won wide congressional approval in 1982. This bill made it a crime to identify any intelligence agents publicly—even if there were no proof of intent to harm agents or the national security.

As a condition of employment, CIA agents must sign papers agreeing to submit for agency review material that they want to publish after leaving government service. The agency can delay clearance for long periods of time or can censor sections showing incompetence within the agency but having no bearing on security.

Frank Snepp, a former CIA agent, wrote a book about the fall of Vietnam that was embarrassing to the agency. The book breached no security, but Snepp had not submitted it to the CIA. The government brought suit against him and his case went to the U.S. Supreme Court, which ruled against him. All royalties from his book then had to be turned over to the government and anything he wrote in the future—including notes for college lectures—had to be submitted to the government for approval.

In March 1983, President Reagan issued National Security Directive 84, which George Orwell fans thought aptly titled. For starters, this directive extended CIA standards to large numbers of non-CIA government employees. They would have to sign a lifetime censorship agreement under which all future speeches and writings—including articles, novels, reports, studies, and lecture notes that might in any way reflect knowledge gained in the government—would be submitted for government approval. Once more—*this censorship was to be for life.*

Another provision in this directive was that the government, in its investigation of leaks, could make people with any security clearances take lie-detector tests. This prospect faced some two-and-a-half million federal employees and an estimated million-and-a-half civilian contractors as well.

Most states do not allow the results of lie-detector tests in court. And objective analysts of these tests have found them to be of no value in determining a person's innocence or guilt.

There was something particularly alarming about our highest officials confusing technical voodooism with national security and substituting voodoo rites for individual rights. Officials who believe

"IF THIS THING WORKS, WE CAN
NAIL ANYONE AROUND HERE WE
CATCH TELLING THE TRUTH"

*November 21, 1982*

"THERE'S NO NEED TO GET UPSET,
NANCY—ALL THE CABINET MEMBERS
WILL PROBABLY BE TAKING LIE
DETECTOR TESTS TOO"

*November 24, 1983*

"TELL THE RUSSIANS YOU'LL
NEGOTIATE IF THEY TAKE ONE OF
MY LIE DETECTOR TESTS AND SIGN
ONE OF MY PLEDGES NEVER TO
REVEAL ANYTHING THAT'S
DISCUSSED"

*December 22, 1982*

"WE KNOW YOU HAVE NO
OBJECTION TO THESE, MR. MEESE—
AND YOU WON'T MIND SKIPPING
LUNCHES AND DINNERS WHILE WE
QUESTION YOU"

*January 24, 1984*

in this kind of security could also get their international strategy and military moves from astrologers or daily horoscopes.

Congress finally roused itself to put Directive 84 on hold until April 15, 1985. In election year 1984, the White House then withdrew the directive—but with no assurance that it would not be reimposed during a second Reagan term.

But in June 1984, the General Accounting Office (GAO) released the results of a survey, which showed that at least 164,000 government employees had already signed the lifetime censorship agreements. The GAO said that the actual numbers were probably far higher since some departments provided inadequate information or none at all.

While the administration was pressing its secrecy measures, secret government documents turned up in an odd kind of guarded place: Lorton Reformatory near Washington, D.C. After an inmate had some of these papers delivered to a Washington television station, the newscasters returned the documents to the government and reported the story.

How did the Lorton criminals obtain top secret papers? Well, the State Department's Bureau of Intelligence and Research (headed by a former CIA official) had sent some furniture to the prison. The Bureau had, however, neglected to remove the sensitive papers from a file cabinet.

Twice the State Department officials thought they had recovered all the documents, only to have other papers turn up. What other highly classified papers remained with prisoners or might have been photocopied by one of them was anyone's guess. But the incident put into some perspective the drastic, far-reaching and hysterical "security" measures affecting the press, the public and millions of people dealing with government work. There is much to be said for simple precautions and ordinary common sense.

In its war against the press and in all its fearful obsession with secrecy, the administration produced no evidence of any case where the national security had been harmed.

President Reagan's cry that he was up to his keister in leaks had not been caused by some breach in our defenses. It had been caused

**"THE BERET GIVES YOU A NICE LOW PROFILE"**

*April 25, 1984*

**"KEEP THE PRESS OUT, FIGHT THE FREEDOM-OF-INFORMATION ACT, MAKE EVERYBODY TAKE A LIE-DETECTOR TEST, AND TURN THESE FILES OVER TO INMATES AT THE NEAREST PRISON"**

*November 11, 1983*

by a news story disclosing that actual Defense Department estimates of Pentagon program costs were considerably higher than those it put out for congressional and public consumption. And a government official about to be axed as the suspected leaker of that story was spared only because George Wilson, *The Washington Post*'s highly respected Defense Department correspondent, wrote a letter stating that the suspect had not been his source.

The Justice Department—which under Attorney General William French Smith had done nothing to fend off attacks on the First Amendment—itself made an unusual attack on the First Amendment in January 1984. It went to court to obtain a restraining order preventing a law book company from publishing, in a hard-cover edition of Federal Court decisions, a federal judge's opinion—already printed in paperback. The reason the Justice Department wanted the restraining order was that the judge, in delivering his opinion, had criticized some Justice Department attorneys.

The administration came in for wider criticism on another policy. Its "covert" activities in Central America provoked the press and Congress, which spoke up against the CIA-sponsored military activities against Nicaragua. These paramilitary operations constituted a kind of open-secret war—conducted by the same agency that brought us the Bay of Pigs.

But the military action that touched off explosions in the press was the invasion of the island of Grenada in October 1983.

The press was completely excluded from the operation and for three days was kept from the island itself. Then small groups of correspondents, accompanied by military escorts, were taken to Grenada for afternoon visits and removed before nightfall.

Two correspondents who succeeded in getting to Grenada during the first days asked to use U.S. communications facilities; and for this purpose they were helicoptered to the U.S.S. Guam offshore. But Vice Adm. Joseph Metcalf III, in charge of the invasion, refused them permission and they were thus kept incommunicado on the ship. Later, they were flown to Grenada ostensibly to watch a military operation—which had already taken place. They were then helicoptered to Barbados and public phones.

Other correspondents in boats were buzzed by military aircraft;

**BACK TO THE CAVE**
*October 21, 1983*

**"NOT THOSE LEAKS, DUMMY—THE LEAKS OF INFORMATION *ABOUT* THEM"**
*February 11, 1982*

**"HE BELIEVES IN PRIVATE INITIATIVE AND PRIVATE GOVERNMENT"**
*April 19, 1983*

**COVERED WAGONS**
*January 26, 1982*

and Metcalf made a straight-faced threat to fire on any boats of press people trying to reach Grenada. This unprecedented situation was summed up succinctly and starkly in a column by Haynes Johnson:

> In the invasion of Grenada we are witnessing what is probably the first "official" war in the history of the United States, produced, filmed, and reported by the Pentagon, under the sanctions of the president. It is a "good" war, conceived in secrecy and carried out in the shadows. All we know about it is "positive," because that is all we are told about it. This goes far beyond war-time censorship of the past. If there has been a comparable total blackout of coverage of a U.S. military engagement on a foreign shore, it does not come to mind.

The administration gave two reasons for its news blackout. One was to maintain secrecy and the other, explained by Secretary of Defense Caspar Weinberger, was that the services could not provide enough personnel to ensure the safety of camera crews and other news people. Both excuses collapsed in the face of facts about all previous American military engagements.

Many correspondents were privy to secrets as they covered the Vietnam War, but they violated no trust.

Among the best-kept secrets of any war were the time and locations of the D-Day landings in World War II. The newsmen who accompanied the troops in landings and parachute drops kept the secrets safe. In many cases they took military secrets to early graves under deadly enemy fire.

Members of the press took part in the landings on Pacific islands under heavier fire than the Caribbean has ever known. The toll of reporters and photographers in our military operations comprise a long honor roll. The Reagan administration's supposed concern for the safety of news people literally added insult to injury.

When Secretary of Defense Weinberger was asked about the complete exclusion of the press, he cited safety reasons and the wishes of the military commander of the invasion: "The reason is of course the commander's decision, and I certainly don't ever, wouldn't ever, dream of overriding commanders' decisions in charge of an operation like this."

This Secretary of Defense never seemed to dream of overriding any decision or request by anybody in what President Eisenhower had called "the military-industrial complex."

In October 1983, when asked about covert activities in Central America, President Reagan said that "while your people may have a right to know, you can't let your people know without letting the wrong people know, those that are in opposition to what you're doing." Assuming that he was referring to potential enemies and not the American press, the Grenada invasion proved once more that secrets often kept from our people are not secret from the "wrong people."

Radio monitoring in the Caribbean, statements by Caribbean country officials, and Reagan orders to send marines from Lebanon to Grenada showed that even though Americans were not aware of the impending invasion, Cuba, Grenada and other governments were.

Secretary of State George Shultz was not ambiguous about who he thought the wrong people were. In a statement on the press, he made an amazing comparison between Grenada and World War II —when the United States defended itself against Japanese attacks and a declaration of war by Adolf Hitler. Shultz said that in World War II "reporters were involved all along. And on the whole, they were on our side." He went on to say that now "It seems as though the reporters are always against us . . . they're always seeking to report something that's going to screw things up."

In referring to "our side" he apparently meant administration officials who regard themselves as the United States. It can only be pointed out that Franklin D. Roosevelt, who believed in a free press, was on "our side"—the side of traditional American rights and values. Mr. Shultz, Mr. Weinberger and Mr. Reagan could have benefited from being on that side, too.

Reagan went a step further and deeper. In reference to the press he said that "beginning with the Korean conflict, and certainly in the Vietnam conflict, there was more criticizing of our forces and what we were trying to do, that it didn't seem that there was much criticism leveled at our enemy." But as columnist Tom Wicker noted, the sharpest criticism of the Truman administration's conduct of the

Korean "conflict" was "leveled" by the Republican Party. It might also be mentioned that neither the actions in Korea or Vietnam followed congressional declarations of war.

The widespread reaction to the anti-press policy in Grenada was illustrated in a February 1984 speech by Herbert Klein, editor-in-chief of the Copley Newspapers. As the former communications director of the Nixon administration, he was no stranger to government-press relations or to concern for secrecy. Describing Grenada as a "major bobble" by the Reagan administration, Klein said that "it seems determined to prove it has a straight line to the truth" and there is a feeling of " 'only we can tell you the truth and the media which doesn't follow our line of thought will be punished.' " Klein said he had advised the Reagan White House that the Grenada blackout was a bad idea.

But in October 1983, the invasion, covered exclusively by the Pentagon, seemed like a complete propaganda success. The Defense Department films of Americans in Grenada welcoming U.S. troops looked fine on television, as did later network shots of "rescued" American students with the president at the White House. Earlier, when those students were being returned to the United States, some of them, apparently in high spirits, kissed the ground while smiling GIs watched. An astute colleague of mine said, "It's all over—that's it—that's the picture people will remember."

She was right, as opinion polls soon indicated, and as a camera-conscious administration must have figured in its scenario. But in real life, everything doesn't stop when a director says "Cut!"

Operation Grenada (working title: *Urgent Fury;* later released as *Rescue Mission*) is worth a closer look than it got in the official script.

■

# ISLAND IN THE SUN

When it comes to travel, I am not one to seek uncharted seas and untrod shores. Cabs, airports, baggage, and hotels are about as much as I care to cope with. Getting to a place that is reasonably comfortable but where I will not be hailed as the one-millionth tourist to arrive that year is about as far off the beaten path as I generally go.

It was in this bounded spirit of adventure that I planned to visit Grenada some time before it left the British nest in 1974, and I reluctantly waited for an island-hopping plane that would take me there. My reluctance was due to the fact that this plane was apparently a sometime thing, and the local airline agent could give no assurance that it would fly as scheduled or that I would be aboard if it did fly. But the thought of wrestling baggage one more time begat a patience that eventually got me on the plane.

I arrived at the small Grenadian airport (Pearls) thinking that a larger landing field might make the island more accessible if less exotic. My stay was pleasant and the only danger came from smiling taxi drivers who regarded fares across the somewhat mountainous terrain as opportunities to take part in an imaginary Grand Prix.

Later I came across occasional and increasingly troubling news items about Grenada: the 1974 election of Prime Minister Eric Gairy;

94

the 1979 coup by Maurice Bishop; and the October 1983 coup, in which Bishop was held captive, freed by supporters and then killed by the military.

Soon after this, Grenada became big news. On the morning of Oct. 25, 1983, I flipped on the TV to see President Reagan and Prime Minister Mary Eugenia Charles, of neighboring Dominica, talk to reporters about the landing on Grenada that morning of "forces from six Caribbean democracies and the United States." Said President Reagan, "Let me repeat, the United States objectives are clear: to protect our own citizens, to facilitate the evacuation of those who want to leave, and to help in the restoration of democratic institutions in Grenada."

The American invasion of Grenada took place two days after the disastrous loss of lives of U.S. Marines in Beirut.

A few days later President Reagan went on television again—this time for a speech covering both situations, which he said were "closely related." He said about Grenada that there were some 1,000 American citizens (800 of them students at a medical school) and that our government had a responsibility to go to the aid of its citizens "if their right to life and liberty is threatened." And "The nightmare of our hostages in Iran must not be repeated."

He said that secrecy was vital for the safety of the mission and "the Americans they were about to rescue."

A little later in his speech, Reagan said, "We got there just in time."

*Whew!*

Also—*Whoa!* Hold on a minute.

After the invasion and a visit to Grenada by a U.S. congressional delegation, Ronald V. Dellums (D-Calif.) said that "our delegation could not find one confirmed instance in which an American was threatened or endangered before the invasion. In fact, the Grand Anse campus was a mere 20 meters from an unprotected beach. If the safety of the students was the primary goal, why did it take the U.S. forces three days to reach it?"

The log released by the Pentagon showed the time of the troops' arrival at the campus as 35 hours after the invasion. In either case, the point is the same. There was plenty of opportunity for the

**"WAIT—I HAVEN'T CAUGHT UP YET WITH THE LATEST EXPLANATIONS ABOUT THOSE OTHER PLACES"**

*October 26, 1983*

**"—WITH ONLY A FEW LOSSES—"**

*October 28, 1983*

**"WHERE ELSE CAN WE SEND THEM?"**

*October 27, 1983*

**SHOWING THE FLAG**

*October 30, 1983*

Grenadian government to threaten lives or take captives. Nothing of the kind occurred.

Despite a shoot-to-kill curfew that had followed the government coup, school officials found no eagerness on the part of the students to leave and no threats to them. In later televised interviews with students, perhaps one of the most significant statements came from a young woman who was asked if she had been scared. She said, "Not until we heard the shooting." The shooting began when our forces arrived.

In speaking about the invasion, President Reagan not only cited the supposed threat to Americans but also said we were acting in response to a request by "the Organization of Eastern Caribbean States, joined by Jamaica and Barbados," that we "join them in a military operation to restore order and democracy to Grenada."

Sol Linowitz, former ambassador to the Organization of American States, wrote a newspaper article on the invasion, in which he cited violations of U.S. hemisphere treaty commitments. And he asked, "What evidence is there . . . that in the few days since the assassination of former Prime Minister Maurice Bishop the danger to the lives of Americans had become so great and their safety so imperiled that this kind of action had to be undertaken? By the same token, if we had convincing evidence that American citizens were truly in danger, why was it necessary for us to await a request from the Organization of Eastern Caribbean States to rescue our fellow citizens?"

President Reagan and others tried to justify the intervention in Grenada by raising the possibility of another Iranian hostage situation. But the two were not comparable.

Many of those who talked about a Vietnam Syndrome seemed to be suffering from an Iranian Hostage Syndrome.

In the Ayatollah Khomeini's Iran we were dealing with a large, well-armed country, one controlling important oil supplies, and— most importantly—located next to Russia. Our government was understandably reluctant to use the kind of force that might bring the U.S.S.R. to Iran's defense or into Iran itself.

The situation in Grenada was entirely different. What possible purpose would it have served a government on this tiny island to

**"ISN'T THIS BETTER THAN ALL
THOSE NEWS STORIES YOU GET
FROM THE PRESS?"**
*November 16, 1983*

**MAN ON FOOT**
*November 1, 1983*

**"AND HERE'S ANOTHER YOUNG MAN
WHO WILL TESTIFY THAT HE WAS IN
DANGER UNTIL THE PRESIDENT
RESCUED HIM"**
*November 8, 1983*

invite a war with the United States—a power that could credibly threaten to wipe out the entire government of that island if a single American was harmed?

British Prime Minister Margaret Thatcher, who did not support the invasion, pointed out that if we were going to go into any country "where communism reigns against the will of the people," then "we are really going to have terrible wars in the world."

The same thing could be said in spades about the fear of hostages being taken. There are U.S. citizens in lots of troubled areas. Thousands of Americans continued to stay in Libya even after our country broke relations with the government of Col. Muammar Qaddafi. While the United States mined the harbors of Nicaragua and took part in a not-so-covert war against its government, we continued to maintain an embassy there.

If we were to invade any country where hostages could conceivably be taken, we'd be at war with countries all over the world.

In speaking of a Grenadian threat, President Reagan also said that the late Maurice Bishop "sought the help of Cuba in building an airport, which he claimed was for tourist trade but which looked suspiciously suitable for military aircraft including Soviet-built long-range bombers."

You have to listen carefully to these things. Were long-range Russian bombers there? Was this a military airport? Not exactly. It "looked suspiciously suitable" for military planes.

Cubans were indeed helping to build the new airport at Point Salines. Observers who had followed the story of Grenada noted that our government had cold-shouldered the idea of aiding the Bishop government with such projects and had even tried to isolate it. Other countries—some free and some not so free—did help.

British contractors responsible for the airport construction pointed out that it was not designed with features required in a military airport. The financing of the construction was done partly with British funds—not very bloody likely for a terrorist base.

There are interesting ironies in the rest of the Point Salines airport story. The first planes to use it *were* war planes—ours. And they might have damaged the unfinished runway. But no problem. In February 1984, the U.S. government decided to pay $21 million toward the completion of the airport.

A study showed that the planned runway was not 10,000 feet long (which would accommodate Soviet and Cuban military planes) but was only 9,000 feet long and comparable to other runways for large tourist planes. The reason for completing the airport was that it was important to the economy of Grenada—which was what the government of Grenada had said at the beginning.

So work proceeded on the new and larger airport that would make it easier to get to Grenada—and a little harder to trust the next "just in time" intervention of our government.

The old Pearls airport, the one still operating in October 1983, also figured in the stories about the invasion. The White House told us the airport was closed at the time of the invasion and so it was impossible to evacuate the Americans. But *The New York Times* interviewed a former Reagan administration official who said he had flown out of Grenada on a chartered plane on the morning of Monday, Oct. 24 (the day before the invasion). Other charter flights left that same morning, when the four-day curfew had been lifted.

Additionally, Canadian embassy officials reported that they knew of several flights in and out of Pearls airport on Monday. Difficulty in flying to nearby islands had resulted from *those* islands canceling flights to and from Grenada.

The many inaccurate, misleading and downright false statements connected with this brief invasion are remarkable—or would be if it were not for the fact that the administration had made it a point to exclude press reporting.

The U.S. State Department had reported to the press the discovery of a mass grave containing over 100 bodies. It later said that this could not be confirmed. A U.S. spokesman on Grenada had, in fact, denied it.

A senior administration official said after the invasion that there were no known civilian casualties. But we later learned that on the very first day of the invasion many had been killed in the bombing of a civilian mental hospital.

President Reagan told the nation of warehouses of military equipment and "weapons and ammunition stacked almost to the ceiling, enough to supply thousands of terrorists." But when newspapermen were eventually taken on escorted tours, they found three of the warehouses contained food, uniforms and engine parts for vehicle maintenance.

The principal storage shed, wrote Loren Jenkins of *The Washington Post,* "was not 'stacked almost to the ceiling' but was probably a quarter full—about 190 crates of assorted guns. Some were modern Soviet-made infantry weapons, but many were antiquated, of little value to a modern army or guerrilla force." And "none of the three warehouses containing the weapons and ammunition supplies was more than half full."

The military supplies, incidentally, had been brought in by the government of Maurice Bishop, who had been in office long before the American invasion that was supposedly triggered by his assassination. If the object was to eliminate this "terrorist base," why did we wait until Bishop was overthrown?

In his speech on the invasion, President Reagan said, "We had to assume that several hundred Cubans working on the island could be military reserves. As it turned out, the number was much larger and they were a military force."

But the facts were different, as Stuart Taylor Jr. reported in *The New York Times* in a comprehensive roundup of official misinformation. He found that the Reagan figures were further exaggerated by Adm. Wesley L. McDonald, who said captured documents showed there were at least 1,100 Cubans on Grenada, all "well-trained soldiers . . . impersonating construction workers." McDonald also said 638 Cubans had been captured and 300 to 350 apparently remained at large. But, wrote Taylor:

> Then last Sunday, the State Department acknowledged that the estimate of 784 Cubans on the island that the Cuban government had given earlier was about right. And on Wednesday, United States military authorities in Grenada said most of the Cuban prisoners had been classified after interrogation as workers, with only about 100 combatants.

Some abbreviated versions of other official misinformation reported by Taylor include these:

● Adm. McDonald told of a "terrorist training base," where, he said, the Cubans planned to put 341 more officers and 4,000 more reservists as part of a Cuban takeover. Later reports indicated that the Cubans had planned to send 27 military advisers to train Grenadian troops.

• Reagan had said that the Soviet Union "has assisted and encouraged the violence" in Grenada and "it is no coincidence that when the thugs tried to wrest control of Grenada, there were 30 Soviet advisers there." A senior administration official was quoted as attributing the killings of Bishop and others to a Soviet-backed assassination team. No evidence was presented of a Soviet or Cuban role in the killings—which Cuban president Fidel Castro had denounced.

• Defense Secretary Caspar Weinberger had said there were "indications" from "intelligence reports" of plans to take American hostages. Intelligence sources later said there was no clear evidence of such a threat.

• The date originally given for the planning of the invasion was Oct. 22, when a request was reported to have been made to the United States by the Organization of Eastern Caribbean States. U.S. officials later said the planning began earlier.

Prime Minister John M. G. Adams of Barbados said that on Oct. 15 one of his aides had been approached by an American official who offered help in launching an operation to rescue Bishop (the jailed prime minister of Grenada). Other statements, including one from the U.S. ambassador to France, indicated that the United States planned the invasion even before the overthrow of Bishop.

• When asked about Bernard Coard, deputy prime minister of Grenada, who helped lead the coup, Vice Adm. Joseph Metcalf III said that Grenadians had captured Coard. Confronted with the fact that the U.S. Marines had captured Coard, Metcalf conceded that he had known this all along.

• Pentagon reports of the number of Americans killed more than doubled after a few days, although most of the casualties took place on the first day.

The Defense Department's final figures on casualties were: 18 U.S. servicemen killed, 116 wounded; 24 Cubans killed, 59 wounded; 45 Grenadians killed and 337 wounded. Twenty-four Grenadian civilians were killed. Seven U.S. helicopters were destroyed and 11 were damaged.

Most of the justifications given for the invasion were ex post facto. But despite the captured arms and documents, the administration never presented evidence of the "terrorist base" it had talked of.

Shortly after the invasion, when President Reagan returned to the White House from a brief trip out of town, he was greeted by applauding staff members. With unconscious irony, one of them carried a sign that read "Your Finest Hour"—a phrase borrowed from Churchill's description of Britain standing alone against the most powerful war machine in the world.

One former government official observed that the U.S. invasion of Grenada was like Notre Dame vs. the Little Sisters of St. Mary's.

In March 1984, it was disclosed that the U.S. Army had awarded to Americans involved in the invasion a total of 8,612 medals—over 1,600 more than the actual number of army troops who were in Grenada. Some of the medals went to people in the Pentagon and others to rear-area support personnel at Army bases in the United States. Army officials defended this depreciation of the currency of medals as a "valuable tool to build unit morale and esprit." There was no report on the morale or esprit of U.S. combat troops, of whom it might be said that they got their medals the old-fashioned way— they earned them.

It was not hard to see why the Grenada operation was a popular success, or at least a public-relations triumph. After the losses and failure in Vietnam, the humiliation in Khomeini's Iran and the military disaster in Lebanon there was satisfaction in feeling that we won one! And against a Marxist regime.

The Reagan administration also temporarily "won one" against the press—at a considerable loss of credibility. The people of Grenada and some of their Caribbean neighbors were reported to be happier after our intervention than they were with the recent government of the island. But things that might not concern the friendly people of the area should concern us—the misinformation put out by our government, the excuses that didn't wash and the precedents of fighting "official" wars in which the public was excluded from the decisions and the actions.

The future of that island may have become brighter. But the invasion remained under a cloud. ∎

Photo Opportunity Album

AID TO PUBLIC SCHOOLS   UNEMPLOYMENT

HOUSING FOR THE POOR   JOB PROGRAMS

SCHOOL LUNCHES   FOOD STAMPS

©1982 HERBLOCK

*May 30, 1982*

# UNTO EVERYONE
# THAT HATH

All of our currency bears the words "In God We Trust." In 1955 Congress decreed that. I've never been sure about the tie-up between God and money. It's a little like saying, Believe in the Lord, but don't forget the cash—as if the reference to a Supreme Being made the dollar a little more Almighty. The word LIBERTY is on our coins but not on our folding money. Maybe the people who decide these things considered Liberty to be comparatively small change. On the coins bearing the likenesses of George Washington, Thomas Jefferson, Abraham Lincoln and Franklin D. Roosevelt, Liberty gets at least equal billing with the religious motto—which might have pleased these presidents.

Our currency, which combines money, religion and political figures—albeit great ones—seems pertinent to the times.

With the rise of fundamentalist religious broadcasting—costing millions of dollars and bringing in millions more—money and religion have become closer than they were in the days when most of the giving was done via collection plates. And both Religion and Money have become more closely associated with Politics. Pray-TV is big business—with big political clout.

**"KOOK-A-DOODLE-DOO!"**
*November 11, 1980*

**"NOW HEAR THIS!—"**
*July 22, 1981*

**"YOU CALL THIS A BILL OF RIGHTS?
WHAT ABOUT THE FOUNDING
FETUSES!"**
*August 5, 1981*

**"ABORTIONS ARE SOMETHING
BETWEEN YOU AND YOUR DOCTOR
AND YOUR LOCAL LOAN SHARK"**
*July 2, 1980*

In a match that might have been made in political heaven, the Rev. Jerry Falwell, fundamentalist "religious right" broadcaster, was an ally of President Reagan.

While professing not to give political endorsements, in 1980 Falwell found the Republican presidential candidate's "pro-family" ideas satisfactory. And Falwell said that vice-presidential candidate Walter Mondale acknowledged being a universalist and "his family roots are humanitarian. Humanitarianism is in my opinion glossed-over atheism."

It's interesting that fervent religious fundamentalists, whether here or in the Ayatollah Khomeini's Iran, find "secular humanists" beyond the pale. The late commentator Elmer Davis once wrote that in the United States we have a kind of secular religion—"a faith in freedom."

For more than 200 years that faith, which embraces people of all religions and those with none at all, has been the great unifying belief in our country.

Reagan shared many religious and political views with Moral Majority Leader Falwell, who in 1984 claimed more than 6 million members. They both:

- Opposed the Equal Rights Amendment.
- Supported a constitutional amendment for organized prayer in the public schools.
- Supported a constitutional amendment to outlaw abortion.
- Supported a policy to require clinics receiving federal funds to notify parents when their under-age daughters sought prescription birth-control aids.
- Supported "creationism"—the teaching of the biblical version of creation—defined in several states as a "science" to counter the teaching of evolution. Reagan believed creationism should be given equal time.
- Opposed the nuclear freeze movement and spoke of the arms buildup as a kind of holy crusade.

**"IN THIS SCIENTIFIC EXPERIMENT, JONAH . . . "**

*December 11, 1981*

*November 25, 1982*

**"BRRR—THAT'S COLD"**

*May 4, 1983*

**ENOUGH!**

*September 11, 1981*

Many other religious groups found that buildup unholy.

In 1982, U.S. Roman Catholic bishops challenged U.S. nuclear policy. And the following year they issued a pastoral letter calling for a halt to the testing, production and deployment of new nuclear weapons. Reagan, who found this kind of religious political action not so appealing, spoke often against such resolutions.

In March 1984, he was applauded by the National Association of Evangelicals when he addressed them. He called nuclear policy a moral issue and "In your discussions of the nuclear freeze proposals I urge you to beware the temptation of pride." This injunction obviously was directed at those clerics inside the hall and outside, who disagreed with his policies.

At that same meeting a speaker said with fervor, "There is sin and evil in the world and we are enjoined by scripture and the Lord Jesus to oppose it with all our might." That speaker was not Rev. Falwell or one of the other professional evangelists. It was the same president of the United States, Ronald Reagan.

Other presidents have expressed a belief in God, but no other president had in effect hit the sawdust trail for a particular brand of religion.

When Theodore Roosevelt spoke of the presidency as being a "bully pulpit" he meant what his cousin Franklin Roosevelt would later call "a position of moral leadership." The Reagan evangelical approach was something new. Of course, Reagan generously urged tolerance for people of other religious faiths.

At the beginning of 1984, Reagan made 10 references to God in his State of the Union message, and mentioned Him 24 times in a speech to the National Association of Religious Broadcasters. Noting this, one White House correspondent observed that Reagan seemed to have made God the honorary chairman of his re-election campaign.

Putting prayer in the schools seemed to get a good response in polls, and Reagan let out all the stops in advocating it. He spoke of God as having been "expelled" from the public schools, and demanded that we let our children "have the right to call on a little help from God at the beginning of their school day." He said that for too long "fundamental American values have been under attack." He may have meant fundamentalist values.

"WHO NEEDS MONEY? YOU GET
YOURSELF A BIRCH STICK AND
WHOP SOME EDUCATION INTO 'EM"
*January 25, 1984*

"HOW ABOUT SOMETHING LIKE
THIS?"
*November 19, 1981*

*January 12, 1983*

*June 16, 1983*

Reagan was not just for organized prayer but for organized *vocal* prayer in the public schools. None of that silent stuff that's just between an individual and God—the kind of thing that school kids, or grownups, can do any time anywhere. Reagan also expressed his belief in the force of many praying at once—as if all American kids praying aloud in unison might have averted the results of bad policy in Lebanon.

The words used in these presidential exhortations were interesting. He was for "voluntary prayer" to give children the same "right" as members of Congress—to open their day with prayer. But does anyone think that peer-conscious children participating in organized prayer under the eye of a teacher can be compared to adults? Grownups can choose whether or not to drop in to a place where prayer is being conducted—and whether they will participate. As for members of Congress, many are not present for an opening prayer—and they do not do any reciting.

Reagan said that God had been "expelled" from our schools. That word rang a school bell with me. As a kid, it was one of the most dread words. It meant something awful—beyond being taken to the principal's office. When Reagan talked about God having been expelled, that sounded as if His deportment was so incorrigibly bad that He had been given His last chance with the principal; and when no justifying note was received from His Father or Mother, He had been *expelled*. I always thought He was somehow bigger than that.

I went to public schools in Chicago, Ill., and I wonder what kind of schools Reagan attended in Dixon, Ill., that were so much different and so much more religious than mine. We never had prayers in the grade schools and the high school I attended. If a teacher had tried to conduct prayer sessions, the PTA members probably would have wanted to know why she wasn't devoting her time to teaching the subjects she was supposed to teach. At the schools I went to, maybe they never let God in. Maybe they barred Him at the door. But none of us ever thought that we couldn't pray to Him any time we wanted, without somebody organizing a prayer for us to recite.

As a matter of fact, when I went to school, the only thing we recited (besides schoolwork) was the Pledge of Allegiance—and God hadn't yet been put into that. But those public schools taught a lot

**TEACHER'S AIDE**

*March 2, 1984*

**"MONEY IS NOT THE ANSWER—
EXCEPT FOR PRIVATE SCHOOLS"**

*July 6, 1983*

**"I WAS JUST THINKING—THE WAY
THINGS HAVE BEEN GOING UNDER
THIS ADMINISTRATION, MAYBE WE
*OUGHT* TO HAVE THE KIDS PRAY"**

*May 10, 1983*

**"YOU SHOULD GIVE THAT ONE A
RAISE"**

*June 23, 1983*

of Americans about democracy and freedom and religious liberty and respect for others. Nobody told us that God hadn't been let in. We thought we could pray to Him at home or in church or in study hour or any time—even when hoping we wouldn't be called on before the bell rang.

I keep wondering what they were doing at Ronald Reagan's school downstate—or what they were teaching him that produced his evangelical fervor as president.

People who win highest office—like lone survivors of disasters—must be tempted to feel that they were singled out for some Divine Purpose. The old phrase *vox populi, vox dei*—"the voice of the people is the voice of God"—may sound literally true to an elected winner. From there, it's just a short step to believing that those with other political or policy views are in opposition to Divine Will.

Such interpretations of God's purpose recall a line in the movie "Patton." The general says, "I feel that God has destined that I should play a great role in this war. *His* will be done."

Famous broadcaster Edward R. Murrow closed his programs with "Good night and good luck"; President Reagan closed his with "Good night and God bless you." When a person becomes very wealthy or rises to very high place in government, maybe it's hard for him to believe that this was largely due to luck.

A person who does not believe in good luck does not believe in bad luck either. So then, rich people must deserve to be rich; if people are poor, they must be doing something wrong; it is not the duty of the rich and highly placed to do something about the poor; and the Lord helps those who help themselves.

This is not really the old-time religion. It is the sweeping of our neighbors' needs under a prayer rug. It is the old go-to-church-on-Sunday and to-hell-with-your-neighbor-the-rest-of-the-week idea.

Franklin Roosevelt took the country off the gold standard. What Ronald Reagan did was take it off the Golden Rule standard.

Despite pious concern about our schools and criticism of them, the Reagan administration cut the federal funds that might have helped them. These funds could have been used to increase school facilities and to provide salaries that would make teaching more attractive.

**"IT'S PART OF THE PLAN TO FREE PEOPLE FROM GOVERNMENT INTERFERENCE"**

*April 24, 1981*

**SERMON ON THE MOUNT**
*March 10, 1983*

*June 5, 1983*

"IF YOU HAD PUT YOUR MONEY IN
STOCKS INSTEAD OF FOOD AND
CLOTHES FOR YOUR KIDS—"

*October 10, 1982*

"YOU HAVEN'T HEARD THE LAST OF
ME"

*March 21, 1984*

"BUT YOU DON'T MIND PROVING IT'S
POSSIBLE TO MAKE MONKEYS OUT
OF PEOPLE"

*January 26, 1984*

More than that, Reagan urged spending for tuition tax credits, which would encourage private-school enrollment at government expense.

And what about the children? Did it make them more spiritual to cut school lunch programs that gave many of them a large part of their daily nutrition? Kids do not live by prayer alone.

Most of the cuts in welfare, food stamps and other benefits were hardest on the most helpless—the children. Aid to Families with Dependent Children (AFDC), a favorite administration target, lost $2 billion through federal and state cuts in the first year 1981–82, and another $85 million in 1983–84.

While the number of children living in poverty increased by more than 1 million between 1981 and 1982, those on AFDC dropped by over 550,000.

In 36 states, even the combined AFDC and food stamp level for a family of three was less than 75 percent of the 1983 poverty level.

In a 1984 book, the *Children's Defense Fund* cited some figures:

- Children are the poorest age group in America. Today, nearly 40 percent of all poor people are children and the number of poor children has been growing steadily.
- The nutritional status of poor children has declined. Child hunger, virtually eliminated by the federal food programs during the 1970s, has returned to communities all over America. Epidemic unemployment exacerbated by massive federal food program cutbacks over the last three years has contributed to this tragedy.
- School Lunch, School Breakfast, Child Care Food and Summer Food programs have been reduced 29 percent or over $5 billion over fiscal years 1982 to 1985.
- The number of children receiving school lunches each day has fallen by nearly 3 million.
- The number of low-income children getting free or reduced-price lunches dropped by nearly one million.
- Nearly 2,700 schools eliminated their school lunch programs.
- One-half million fewer children participate in the School Breakfast Program.
- Day care centers and homes may now serve a child two rather than three meals, and one rather than two snacks a day regardless of whether they are in care more than eight hours.
- 400,000 fewer poor children receive summer lunches.
- One million recipients have been dropped from the Food

**"FREEZE!"**

*February 1, 1983*

**"BARGAINING CHIPS"**

*May 31, 1983*

**"OF COURSE, NOT ALL THE PEOPLE
WE DROPPED FROM THE ROLLS
WOULD GET BACK ON"**

*April 5, 1984*

**"LOOK AT IT THIS WAY—YOUR
GLASS IS HALF FULL"**

*September 10, 1981*

Stamp Program. Twenty million have had their benefits reduced. . . . Half of all food stamp beneficiaries are children.

In addition: "Health care access for poor children and mothers has been severely eroded."

As for the unemployed:

"Fifty percent of all families experiencing unemployment receive no federal assistance: 82.8 percent receive no food stamps, and 60 percent receive no unemployment insurance."

And—

"The fiscal 1985 Reagan administration budget proposes to cut another $3 billion . . . more from programs designed to help poor, handicapped homeless and minority children and families."

When it came into office in 1981, the Reagan administration even cut the highly successful Head Start program, but Congress restored some of the funds.

An administration that set itself up as a champion of the unborn and had little enthusiasm for family planning could at least have shown more concern for children already born.

One of the Reagan administration's most cruel cuts was in benefits to the disabled. Beginning in March 1981, the administration disqualified countless disability victims who had shown no improvement and in some cases were bedridden or too crippled to fight to retain their benefits. In March 1984, the House of Representatives was sufficiently outraged that it voted—by 410 to 1—for a Social Security disability program amendment that would provide for fair review of cases.

In April 1984, the Congressional Budget Office issued a study showing that, as the old saying goes, the rich get richer and the poor get poorer. Taxes for high-bracket incomes went down, corporation taxes dwindled to near zilch and Reagan proposed abolishing corporation taxes altogether.

Those who used to be awed by the term "millionaire" found that people with total assets of a million dollars had become small potatoes. What we had now was a new kind of millionaire—people with incomes of more than a million a year. They comprised a long list, with many making several millions a year. Talk about gross incomes!

**"I'M IN THE SAME AGE BRACKET AS YOU"**

*December 4, 1981*

**"I TOLD YOU THE PRICE STICKERS WERE ENOUGH!"**

*May 6, 1984*

**"HE RUNS OUT OF SUPPLIES BEFORE HE GETS TO OUR SIDE"**

*April 6, 1982*

**THE SEARCH FOR WASTE, FRAUD AND ABUSE**

*November 2, 1983*

While programs for the poor were being slashed, Reagan friends appointed to federal positions lived in high style. At taxpayers' expense, they had to have the costliest hotel rooms. When they traveled, they needed special flights, and some felt they had to be accompanied by their spouses.

In 1982 Attorney General William French Smith took a 23-day trip around the world, ostensibly to campaign against drugs, at a cost to the taxpayers of more than $683,000. His wife accompanied him on the trip, as did 16 Justice Department officials, 11 FBI agents and six officials from the State Department and other agencies.

Reagan urged that the poor and unemployed be assisted through private charity and old-fashioned neighborly help. But the days of friendly rural neighbors helping with a barn-raising are light years away from today's vast city slums, where unemployment runs high and food and hopes run low—and the neighbors are in no position to help.

As for charity, columnist Mary McGrory asked President Reagan about it at a January 1982 press conference:

> **Q:** Mr. President, in New York last week, you called upon the rich to help the poor in this present economic difficulty. Are you planning to increase your own contributions to private charity to set an example to the rich people of this country to do more for the poor?
>
> **A:** No, Mary, I tell you, you give me a chance to explain something that has been of great concern to me. I realize the publicity that has intended upon the tax returns of someone in my position. And I realize that some have noticed that there seemed to be a small percentage of deductions for worthwhile causes and that is true. And I'm afraid it will be true this year because I haven't changed my habits but I also happen to be someone who believes in tithing—the giving of a tenth.
>
> But I have for a number of years done some of that giving in ways that are not tax deductible with regard to individuals that are being helped. . . .

Being someone who says he *believes* in tithing and being someone who *tithes* are two different things. Reagan's tax returns never showed that kind of giving.

Readers were free to make their own charitable deductions about other remarks by Edwin Meese and President Reagan.

**"GOT TO LIGHTEN THE CARGO AGAIN
—WOMEN AND CHILDREN FIRST"**
*June 10, 1982*

**"NOW TO FIND OUT WHAT AILS
THOSE PEOPLE"**
*August 3, 1983*

**"GRANTED YOU HAVE STOMACH
PAINS, BUT ARE THEY RAMPANT?"**
*January 10, 1984*

*December 20, 1983*

In December 1983, Meese said that he had never seen "any authoritative figures that there are hungry children in America" and added that some people go to soup kitchens "because the food is free and . . . that's easier than paying for it." Reagan supported Meese's comments in an interview in which he added that "those private groups have no way of checking on the credentials of someone who comes in there."

That was two weeks before Christmas.

On Jan. 9, 1984, the President's Task Force on Food Assistance said it found no substantiation for "reports of rampant hunger," and found very little evidence of "widespread undernutrition." However, it found evidence that many people can't get enough food on occasion. The task force did not recommend large increases in federal spending for food programs—programs that the Reagan administration had cut.

On Jan. 31, 1984, President Reagan spoke of a "problem that we've had . . . the people who are sleeping on the grates, the homeless who are homeless, you might say, by choice."

So—they have made their beds on grates and they can lie on them.

There are indeed many street people, including some mentally disabled, who don't seek roofs over their heads. The trouble begins with the early choices—choosing to be poor, choosing to be disadvantaged, choosing sometimes to be mentally ill. Is the government supposed to help people like that—people who sleep on grates? Unlike the well-to-do who are *entitled* to be rich and to receive government benefits, those poor people who made the wrong choices must be carefully scrutinized.

In an interview a few days later, Reagan returned to his moral theme in a curious statement: "If there are people who suffer from our economic program, they are people who have been dropped from various things like food stamps because they weren't morally eligible for them." Not *in*eligible—but not "morally eligible." These might be incorrigible people who willfully choose to be poor and become a burden to us—or maybe legally eligible recipients who have in some way sinned in the eyes of the Moral Majority. Anyhow, it seems they were dropped because of some "moral" flaw that was not spelled out.

**"YEAH, MAN, THIS SURE BEATS GOING TO A NICE WARM RESTAURANT AND BUYING A REGULAR MEAL"**

*December 14, 1983*

**"STRANGE HOW SOME CHOOSE TO LIVE LIKE THAT INSTEAD OF CHOOSING TO BE RICH LIKE US"**

*February 2, 1984*

**"THE GODS ARE ANGRY"**
*April 12, 1981*

**"IT'S OUR NEWEST MODEL SAFETY NET—THE MACRAME PARACHUTE"**
*February 18, 1982*

**"OUR PRELIMINARY DIAGNOSIS IS THAT YOU'VE BEEN SPOILED ROTTEN"**

*June 22, 1982*

**"SUPPOSE WE TRY SETTING IT ON THE GROUND"**
*July 21, 1982*

In his moral injunctions, President Reagan spoke of "facing the future with the Bible" and said that within it "are all the answers to all the problems that face us today—if we'd only read and believe."

In his March 1984 speech to the National Association of Evangelicals, in which he said that in recent years we seemed to have lost our "religious and moral bearings," he told of "one of my favorite Bible quotations," which came from Second Chronicles:

> If My people who are called by My name humble themselves, and pray and seek My face, and turn from their wicked ways, then will I hear from heaven and forgive their sin and heal their land.

There are so many Bible quotations, it's hard to pick favorites. There is one particularly apt for the organized-prayer debate—Matthew 6:5–6:

> And when thou prayest, thou shalt not be as the hypocrites are: for they love to pray standing in the synagogues and in the corners of the streets, that they may be seen of men. Verily I say unto you, They have their reward.
> But thou, when thou prayest, enter into thy closet, and when thou hast shut thy door, pray to thy Father which is in secret; and thy Father which seeth in secret shall reward thee openly.

That might not have appealed to presidential speech writers if they helped with any selecting—and they would probably skip Matthew 19:24:

> It is easier for a camel to go through the eye of a needle, than for a rich man to enter into the kingdom of heaven.

A good summary of White House economic policy appears in Matthew 25:29 but might not be considered politically advisable for a public speech:

> Unto every one that hath shall be given, and he shall have in abundance; but from him that hath not shall be taken away even that which he hath.

But for highly moral public officials interested in the Christian spirit and holding pencils poised for new cuts in aid to the poor, the disabled and the children, I'd suggest Matthew 25:40:

> Inasmuch as ye have done it unto one of the least of these my brethren, ye have done it unto me.                                    ∎

**"SAY 'CHEESE' "**

*July 18, 1982*

**"CLIMB UP HERE AND LET'S HAVE A LOOK AT YOU"**

*August 7, 1983*

**"REAGAN IS RIGHT! HERE'S PAGE AFTER PAGE OF WANT-ADS: ARCHITECTS, BOOKKEEPERS, COMPUTER PROGRAMMERS, DATA PROCESSORS, EDITORS, EDUCATORS, ENGINEERS . . . "**

*April 22, 1981*

**"WE ALL SUFFER TOGETHER"**

*March 20, 1981*

**"I DIDN'T GET EVERYTHING I ASKED FOR, EITHER"**
*December 21, 1982*

**"RONALD HAS SOME VERY ORIGINAL THOUGHTS"**
*April 28, 1983*

**"VERY WARMING"**
*January 23, 1983*

**"THE ADMINISTRATION HAS AUTHORIZED ME TO TAKE THE HINDMOST"**
*September 18, 1981*

# PRESS CONFERENCE

Good morning, ladies and gentlemen. Please be seated. Before we get to the questions I have a brief opening statement. I was talking with some of my staff members today, and I'm happy to say they tell me that our administration is doing very well and the country is in fine shape. This will be good news to all patriotic Americans who want to see our country do well. It will only displease those purveyors of gloom and doom who inject politics into everything, and who belittle all that is good about America and all that this great country is capable of doing. If they should be elected, our country will once again face the desperate situation that existed when I took office in January 1981.

Inflation was roaring ahead at 36 percent; interest rates were at a staggering 28 percent; 80 million Americans were out of work; and people in other countries were burning the American flag while our government sat idly by, afraid even to lift a finger to burn foreign flags in retaliation—afraid to send our brave U.S. Marines and our battleships to teach those foreign pawns of Moscow a decent respect for the American flag that symbolizes all the hopes and dreams of this nation—what Lincoln called the last best hope of earth.

Since that day in January 1981, when I acted promptly to save the country from total collapse, we proved that, as Franklin Roosevelt said, the only thing we have to fear is fear itself. And as John F. Kennedy warned, we had to get this country moving again. Because we acted quickly and decisively, inflation has been licked, interest rates have come down, and all Americans are better off than they were before.

Today, American flags are no longer being burned. Under the leadership of this administration, America once more stands tall at home and in the world, and as your president, I intend to keep it that way. And now, I know all of you have questions. Helen?

Q: Mr. President, the figures you just gave on the economy and interest rates. They don't seem to jibe with figures we're familiar with. Can you tell us the source of these figures? They sound inflated.

A: No, Helen, inflation is what we have put down. And Helen, I'm a little surprised that a member of the press should raise a question about these figures because I have been told they appeared in a publication—that is, in a part of the press itself. So I think we would all do well to read things other than just what we write ourselves (laughter). I don't mean you, Helen. I don't want anyone to accuse me of having a gender gap (more laughter). Yes—Andrea?

Q: Sir, you said no American flags are now being burned. For several weeks, NBC-TV has been showing foreign demonstrations in which this has been happening.

A: Those were American flags only in a narrow technical sense. Actually, they were made in Japan, which, while it is a friendly country, is not American, and I think the television reporters know that, if they would only tell their viewers and listeners. One of my first actions on taking office was to order that all official American flags at our embassies and so on be made flame-retardant. I also had them Scotchgarded and starched to keep them cleaner and to make them stand out a little straighter in the wind. And there is no instance of any of those flags having been burned successfully, except perhaps for a little scorching around the edges. Yes, Lou?

Q: Sir, when you ran for president, you promised to balance the budget by the end of 1983. But today the budget is more out of balance than ever. Would you comment on that, please?

**A:** I'm glad you asked that question, Lou, because a balanced budget is something I feel strongly about, and we would have it today if only the Democrats in the House of Representatives would give it to us. But they have so far refused to cooperate. However, the door is still open to them, and I am going to try in every way I know how to get them to come up the sidewalk with a balanced budget.

**Q:** If I may, a follow-up, sir. You yourself have never offered a balanced budget. How do you expect Congress . . .

**A:** Lou, you and I have known each other a long time, and we both know that Congress has what I guess the political scientists would call "the power of the purse." And that's a lot of power. But I came here to Washington with a mandate to change things, and I am not going to give up in my efforts to balance the budget, even though Congress might. And when they hear from the people at home, I think some of them will change their minds. Also, I think most people are aware that I strongly favor a constitutional amendment to make sure that future presidents *do* balance the budget instead of leaving us burdened with debt as past presidents have done. Over here—Sam?

**Q:** Sir, the statistics you gave make no mention of unemployment, which I think now stands at about 9 percent. What do you propose to do about that?

**A:** Well, let me say first of all that if there is one person unemployed in this country, it is one too many. But if the policies of past administrations had been followed, and we projected the results of those policies to now, we would today have an unemployment rate of 39 percent. So we have actually achieved a *reduction* of about 30 percent. Furthermore, these unemployed people pay little or no taxes, which lifts from them the burden of overtaxation that I have fought against and successfully. Also those unemployed who still have savings they can draw on will find that reduced inflation has made their savings more valuable, and also there are many good investments that can be made in the stock market today which would increase the value of those savings still more. So we might say that the unemployed never had it so good. And while we are not entirely satisfied with the picture today, it is far brighter than it has ever been before under previous administrations, and as we project our figures into the future, it is even brighter.

**Q:** Sir, a follow-up—the cuts in welfare benefits have apparently been felt by many of the poor. What do you propose to do about that?

**A:** Well, I'm concerned about anyone who is on welfare, that is *legitimately* on welfare. And let me say that if there is one person legitimately on welfare, that is one too many. But I emphasized the word legitimately, because the welfare rolls have been padded, as I have always maintained, and I will give you an example.

I have heard of one woman on welfare who took the change from her food stamps in vodka, then turned around and sold the vodka at exorbitant prices, which she invested in, well—bawdy houses—which are not in line with our thinking about family life *or* fiscal responsibility. And she continued cashing food stamps while owning four grocery stores of her own, three condominiums, four Cadillacs and two laundromats.

So that will give you an idea of how welfare programs were shot through with waste, fraud and abuse, which we came into office to get rid of, despite the doubting Thomases. I don't mean you Helen. I've been neglecting this side of the room. Yes—over here—no behind you—Ann—

**Q:** Sir, there have now been six reports on hunger in America, which show that many people, children in particular, are going hungry today. Will you comment on that?

**A:** Well, to start with, evidence of hunger and that sort of thing is only anecdotal. Whenever you have people who feel they are not getting enough to eat, you are going to hear all kinds of horror stories about "hunger." Of course, if there were actually one person really going hungry in America . . .

**Q:** It would be one too many?

**A:** That's right. And I can tell you that today in America, our farmers are outproducing farmers anywhere in the world—making food abundant in this country. And anyone who can't get enough to eat here should try living behind the Iron Curtain, where people have to line up for hours just to get an orange or a piece of bread. So I think that anyone with American initiative and a will to work is not going to go hungry in this land. Yes?

**Q:** Sir, last night on CBS television they showed some footage of CIA Director William J. Casey and Attorney General William French Smith carrying a small safe out of the Democratic Party headquarters. I wonder if you would comment on that. And a follow-up, if I may.

**A:** Well, as you know, I've had some experience with movies and I know what can be done with cameras. I'll only say that if such a thing actually happened, Bill Casey, as head of the CIA, would not have taken part in it unless it was something necessary to our national security.

**Q:** Sir, do you think that if this did happen, it would call for the appointment of a special prosecutor?

**A:** Well, we're getting into hypothetical cases again. I'll just say that any time a special prosecutor needs to be appointed, I know the attorney general will ask for one—that's his job, and I wouldn't try to second-guess him. But, as I say, this is all speculative and hypothetical, and the fact that some Democratic congressmen have commented on those TV pictures seems to be a pretty clear indication that the Democrats are still playing politics and are up to their same old tricks. Yes—one more question—Lesley?

**Q:** Sir, since your last press conference, four months ago, another 200 American servicemen have been killed in Tierra del Fuego, and 100 more in Northern Ireland. Do you feel that these losses were necessary? Could not these lives have been saved?

**A:** Well, Lesley, let me say first of all that I think you know how I feel about those fighting men over there, and you know they wouldn't be there if it weren't a matter of solemn duty and patriotism, which every one of them feels. But they are there because those areas are of vital interest to the United States—areas that our communist adversaries, who are behind the so-called "liberation movements," covet and would like to add to their empire. So it is a matter of the greatest importance to our country and to the entire free world that they man the ramparts of freedom for all of us and for our children and our children's children and our children's grandchildren and their grandchildren.

I don't need to tell you that the loss of one soldier or sailor or flier or coastguardsman or marine is one too many. And instead of people questioning or criticizing and making things difficult for our brave service people, I think they should all get behind our men who are shouldering the burden over there and give them our prayers. I think God would rather hear those prayers welling up from a great and grateful nation than listen to the nit-picking and criticism from people who are interested only in politics, and who sometimes seem to forget what our nation is all about, and I guess they forget about God, too.

Because I thought this question might come up, I brought along a letter from one of the parents of a man who made the supreme sacrifice, after I wrote a personal letter to each and every one of those parents. I won't go into my letters, which were not important. I just mentioned to them that these dead shall not have died in vain and that this nation under God shall have a new birth of freedom and some things like that I wrote because I felt deeply about them.

This is the letter from Mrs. Milton Machree, of 23 W. 45th St. East, South Selwick, Iowa, 31175: "Dear Mr. President: We want to thank you for your letter and for your prayers. May God bless you too. We know that you wouldn't have sent our boy to die in Tierra del Fuego unless it was necessary to save freedom and everything good in America. We have two more boys helping on the farm, who we are ready to send if you need them. And there is a younger one coming along that we are ready to send too if he does not carry his share of the chores and just keeps on thinking about girls all the time. We pray that you will keep on doing everything you are doing for our country and for freedom and price supports and cutting the capital gains tax and everything. We've seen "Hellcats of the Navy" three times and we know we can always count on you to win. God bless you again sir, and may He smite those godless politicians who oppose you and who never bless us in their speeches and may they be damned forever to burn in eternal hell. God bless you and keep you." And that letter is signed, Mother Machree. Well, that's just one letter, but I think it speaks for all Americans and tells how they feel about keeping our country great and strong and proud.

Q: But sir . . .

Q: Thank you, Mr. President.

A: Golly, the time really slips by. There were a lot of you that had questions I know you wanted to ask and I hope to get to you next time. I guess we'll all have to do a little more fast talking (laughter). See you next year. ∎

"I DIDN'T REALIZE HE'D HAVE SUCH A COMPREHENSIVE
APPROACH TO FOREIGN AFFAIRS"

*May 11, 1984*

# TOUGH STUFF

I don't know what the mattress industry is trying to tell us, but I know a trend when I see one. We used to think of beds as downy soft —to sink into and dream on. But those dreams have been ended by a harsh reality. You know what the mattress ads feature these days? Firm, Extra Firm, Super Firm and Ultra Firm. Whatever happened to soft—or even medium? If we asked, they'd probably say that doctors recommend firmness and it's good for you. Never mind that there used to be choice in these things, just as in diet and exercise.

But eventually the mattress people may do themselves out of business. If harder is better, people might do away with mattresses entirely and sleep on the floor.

This has been a troubling trend because it has seemed to go along with a similar feeling in the Reagan administration that hardness is good, more hardness is better—and reasonable flexibility is sissy. If there were problems with our schools, that was because we weren't hard enough on the kids and the teachers. If people were poor or unemployed, they needed a good kick in the rear to go out and get a job.

There has been a certain selectivity to the toughness.

137

**"DRINKS F'RALL THESE GENTL'M'N—
ANYBODY SAYS HE'S NO FRIEN' OF
RUSSIA IS A GOOD FRIEN' OF MINE"**
*September 4, 1981*

**"WELL, HE WAS PLAYING A
DIFFERENT ROLE THEN"**
*October 27, 1981*

**QUIET DIPLOMACY**
*June 2, 1981*

**"PRETTY SOON OUR EUROPEAN
ALLIES SHOULD SEE THE LIGHT"**
*August 10, 1982*

Domestically, it has not generally been applied to big business interests, and white-collar crime has often been handled with white gloves.

The ultra-firm policy abroad has not applied to all governments run by toughs. It has not applied to right-wing dictatorships, which administration officials dubbed "authoritarian" as distinguished from communist dictatorships, which are "totalitarian." There is a further selectivity even here. Toughness toward communist nations does not apply to a country like China—a nice place for a president to be photographed visiting, but he wouldn't want to live there. Toughness does apply, however, to Russia and to countries suspected of being influenced or aided by Russia—even if the Russian aid has come only after we have ignored the needs of those countries.

In pursuit of this policy, the Reagan administration gave the tough treatment to our European allies for cooperating with the U.S.S.R. in the construction of a Russian natural gas pipeline to Europe. But the pipeline proved stronger than the hard line. And after some hemming and hawing and harrumphing, this tough policy was formally abandoned in May 1983.

Reagan administration supporters claimed that its tough policy toward Russia and Marxist states would produce a climate suitable for negotiations. But the climate never seemed to be just right, so the tough-and-tougher policy continued on. It was something like the giant gorilla a man showed off to a friend on the golf course. The proud owner teed up a ball that the gorilla proceeded to hit 300 yards down the fairway. Amazing! On the next shot the gorilla hit the ball for another 300 yards and it landed on the green. Wonderful! The gorilla then stepped up to the ball, and hit it for another 300 yards.

At some point, a great power needs to know how to putt. In its relations with Russia, the administration did a lot of flailing away in the rough.

Before he became president, Ronald Reagan opposed the arms control agreements and nuclear test ban treaties that previous administrations had negotiated with Russia. Predecessors who had been too soft apparently included virtually all the presidents of the nuclear age—Eisenhower, Kennedy, Johnson, Nixon, Ford and

"WELL—IT'S THE SAME FOREIGN
POLICY I HAD WHEN I WAS
GOVERNOR OF CALIFORNIA"
*June 25, 1981*

"BUT WHAT KIND OF MESSAGES IS
GREAT CHIEF COMMUNICATOR
COMMUNICATING?"
*April 15, 1983*

"HERE IS THE ANSWER—WHAT ARE
YOUR QUESTIONS?"
*September 16, 1981*

"BE SURE TO REMIND THE CHINESE
THAT THE RUSSIANS ARE A BUNCH
OF COMMUNISTS"
*January 21, 1983*

Carter. When, early in his presidency, Mr. Reagan stated that the Soviet leaders "reserve unto themselves the right to commit any crime, to lie, to cheat," the continuation of campaign rhetoric reflected a continuation of policy.

Reagan's hard line achieved a glacial firmness when he spoke to evangelical leaders in March 1983. He cited Russia as an aggressive "evil empire"—and "the focus of evil in the modern world."

Elsewhere he cited Vietnam and Korea as wars we should have won—if only we had used more military power and had not been restrained by fears of expanding those conflicts to the point of confrontations with China or Russia.

These presidential statements sounded chillingly like the gung-ho Reagan rhetoric of earlier years. In October 1965, he said that "We should declare war on North Vietnam. We could pave the whole country, put parking stripes on it and still be home for Christmas."

In all these speeches, there was more than a suggestion that previous administrations had been scaredy-cats, that they did not throw around sufficient tough talk about the U.S.S.R. and that they must have had illusions that the fellows in the Kremlin were sweet guys. Never mind the hair-raising Cuban missile crisis of the Kennedy administration; and never mind the bombs unloaded on North Vietnam by Presidents Lyndon Johnson and Richard Nixon. These were, after all, mere conventional bombs; and besides they were not dropped on the "evil empire" itself.

We did not have to feel trust in the Soviet leaders in order to note that Reagan's constant verbal belting away at them did not advance the cause of arms control, which he professed to want. More than that, his high-decibel rhetoric did not give *other* countries the impression that he really wanted arms control.

His attitude toward past agreements with Russia seemed to resemble Groucho Marx's on private clubs—the kind of club that would have me for a member, I wouldn't want to join. Reagan seemed to feel that any agreements satisfactory to those Russian fellows must be something we shouldn't join in.

In the nuclear age, most people are aware that we need to worry not only about our possible adversaries in Eastern Europe, but also

**"SPECIAL DELIVERY"**

*August 17, 1982*

**CLOUDLAND**

*April 15, 1982*

**PICNIC**

*April 1, 1982*

**SANDBOX**

*August 13, 1982*

about another great power—The Bomb. The Reagan administration's seeming indifference to this caused concern here and among our allies.

In an apparent effort to show how tough we were, administration members such as Secretary of Defense Caspar Weinberger talked of surviving an extended nuclear war in which we must be able to "prevail." And there was not much reassurance in the statement of presidential adviser Edwin Meese on the subject when he allowed that nuclear war was "something that might not be desirable."

Deputy Undersecretary of Defense for Strategic Nuclear Forces T. K. Jones came up with memorable recommendations for civil defense: *Dig a hole. Cover it with a couple of doors and then throw three feet of dirt on top. It's the dirt that does it.* And *Everybody's going to make it if there are enough shovels to go around.*

The Federal Emergency Management Agency (FEMA) offered happy thoughts about orderly evacuations of city people to the country. A trip to the country away from the hurly-burly of city life! Perhaps we could take along a picnic lunch until the nuclear holocaust blew over. Anyone who had ever been in weekend traffic around Washington in the summer or who'd had any experience on a city bridge during rush hours had to wonder what kind of dream world these supposedly hard-headed leaders were living in—and whether they had anything but their warheads screwed on right.

The planners at FEMA also brightly suggested that with the exodus from the cities there should be plenty of farm labor available. Certainly. And the fallout from the bombs might be considered a kind of free crop dusting.

As a further note of reassurance, we were advised that there were plans for postal service to resume following a nuclear exchange, so that we could get ourselves and our whereabouts all sorted out.

Of course, some mail might be returned with a notice that the person was no longer at that address, and neither was the address —or the street—or the post office—or the city.

The mailmen's blue uniforms would presumably be bomb-proofed in some way. They could then complete their appointed rounds, stayed neither by rain nor snow nor heat nor gloom of night—now made bright by radiation.

**"HOW'S THIS FOR SCARING THE RUSSIANS?"**

*October 28, 1981*

**FATHER OF NUCLEAR FREEZE**

*March 16, 1983*

**"I HAVE HERE IN MY HAND—"**

*November 17, 1982*

**"REAGAN SAYS IF WE SPEND ENOUGH MONEY ON ARMS FOR ENOUGH YEARS, WE CAN CLOSE A 'WINDOW OF VULNERABILITY' "**

*January 4, 1983*

All this was evidently supposed to impress the Russians—and us —with the idea that we were ready for anything. After the nuclear blasts, we would brush off the debris, do a John Wayne walk to wherever our six-shooters were hanging, and show them how tough we were. This government bravado made many Americans feel about their leaders the way the Duke of Wellington was said to have remarked about some of his troops: "They may not scare the enemy, but by God, sir, they frighten me."

At one press conference President Reagan observed, in answer to a question, that a nuclear war might be confined to Europe. This had about the same effect on our allies as placing a cat on a hot stove.

When the nuclear freeze movement began growing, a surprised and anguished Reagan declared that participants in it were being "manipulated." The one person who did more than anyone else to create and stimulate the nuclear freeze movement was Reagan himself, whose heated rhetoric activated it just as surely as high temperatures kick on an air conditioner or a sprinkler system.

The Reagan arms policies were based on assertions—also overheated—that the Russians had been arming furiously while our government snoozed. However, the Carter administration had been increasing our arms buildup before Reagan accelerated the rate. The Russian buildup showed a steady increase. But the CIA, in November 1983, revised its previous estimates of Soviet arms spending, finding that those estimates had been at least double the actual amounts. This significant downward change in CIA calculations was rejected by the Defense Department, which kept the alarm bells ringing.

A military comparison of superpower strengths came from a member of the Joint Chiefs of Staff who conceded that he would not trade our arms capability for that of the Kremlin. But President Reagan insisted that the Russians were now militarily superior to us, creating a "window of vulnerability" that required an all-out arms effort.

This open window did not cause a national draft—merely a continuance of a draft registration in case anything were to come through that window.

**"HERE'S THE PLAN—WE WAIT TILL HALLOWEEN, LEAVE IT ON SOMEBODY'S LAWN, AND RUN LIKE HELL"**

*September 2, 1981*

**DENSEPACK**

*August 26, 1982*

**"IT'S OUR LATEST DEPLOYMENT SYSTEM—THE SIXPACK"**

*May 11, 1982*

**"AND *NOW*—THE MXMASTER!"**

*November 10, 1982*

Among the top-priority items called for were the construction and deployment of the MX (for missile experimental) missile. The MX and a deployment plan for it had already been approved by President Carter—one of the predecessors who Reagan implied had left us naked to our enemies. Many plans for deploying these missiles had been considered. One plan, to put them in the silos presently housing old Minuteman missiles, was ruled out because the old silos were considered vulnerable to present-day nuclear weapons. The Carter administration preference was for a "race-track system," in which the missiles would be moved around in an attempt to keep the enemy guessing—a plan ridiculed by Reagan.

The Reagan administration came up with a "dense pack" system, in which the missiles would be massed in such a way that (theoretically) an attack on them would result in the incoming missiles blowing each other up.

Officials of the states that would play host to the missiles failed to appreciate the honor; and the MX deployment problem was finally tossed to a commission headed by Gen. Brent Scowcroft.

The commission's job was to come up with a bipartisan plan for basing the MX. This it did in a report that recommended (hold on to your hat) placing the MX missiles in the old Minuteman silos. Somehow these were to be hardened to make them more resistant to attack.

The commission also recommended the building of small mobile "Midgetman" missiles and emphasized the importance of arms control as well as arms modernization. But these matters seemed to be given low priority by the MX enthusiasts in the government.

The Scowcroft Commission report did something else too. In effect, it closed Reagan's "window of vulnerability" by finding that our defenses were not so inadequate after all.

One of the darkly humorous aspects to the MX planning—besides the thought of all those missiles going around in all those heads and finally coming to rest in the same old silos—was Mr. Reagan's "window." It was calculated that this window would remain open (and we would remain vulnerable) through the 1980s—during which time we would make and deploy lots of new nuclear weapons.

**"I SURE HOPE NOBODY STARTS
ANYTHING SMALL"**

*June 1, 1984*

**"YOURS"**

*September 27, 1983*

**"IT DEMONSTRATES WILL—NOT
BRAINS, MAYBE, BUT WILL"**

*May 11, 1983*

**"BE IT EVER SO HUMBLE . . . "**

*April 17, 1983*

But wait! If the Russians did indeed have the nuclear superiority that Reagan claimed, and if they were so mindlessly evil in their plans to destroy us, why on earth would they wait a few years for us to catch up? Why weren't their missiles already flying through that window—and through all our windows—while our speeches, plans and missiles were being made? The answer would seem to be that they didn't have that superiority and were not that nutty.

Following the Scowcroft report, Reagan made a couple more references to the "window of vulnerability," which was then taken down and stored next to such other worries as Eisenhower's Southeast Asian "domino theory" and John F. Kennedy's 1960 "missile gap."

Along with its tremendous cost, the MX managed to combine vulnerability with provocation. Because it would be an easy target in imperfect silos, it could hardly be used except as a first-strike weapon—and might be an invitation to an enemy first strike. Thus the MX would be either too soon or too late.

The more impressive nuclear deterrents were our mobile weapons —particularly our submarine-launched missiles. As a bargaining chip the MX was not likely to cause the Russians to dismantle *their* land-based missiles, which play a predominant role in their defense plans.

Reagan also came up with his "Star Wars" proposal—a high-in-the-sky, higher-priced, highest-tech "strategic defense initiative" that would supposedly make us invulnerable.

But the history of breakthroughs in new armaments—even when they work—is not exactly encouraging. When President Nixon first deployed the MIRV (multiple warhead) missiles, our technology was supposed to give us a definite edge, as well as another possible "bargaining chip." Now both superpowers have hydra-headed supermissiles capable of hitting many targets at once; and agreements to get back to merely devastating single-warheads would look like a return to the good old days.

Those who approved of the Reagan administration's hell-for-leather buying of all kinds of arms and more and more nuclear missiles liked to think of him as a latter-day Winston Churchill. But

**RACE**
*November 27, 1983*

*August 22, 1982*

**"THAT'S DANGEROUS, THAT TV PROGRAM"**
*November 17, 1983*

**"WE'VE BEEN PRETTY LUCKY SO FAR"**
*September 17, 1981*

when Churchill became prime minister, England's war potential was vastly inferior to that of the Nazis—and nobody had nuclear weapons.

Today these weapons enable each superpower to destroy the other many times over, and very possibly to destroy life on earth. Fortunately, Churchill lived into the nuclear age and also had something to say about overkill. He asked, "Why make the rubble bounce?"

A fictional version of some small-scale rubble was shown in a much-hyped TV film of 1983 titled "The Day After." Among hardliners like evangelical leader Jerry Falwell the showing of a film purporting to display some effects of a nuclear war was dangerous propaganda. And the administration, which had a high regard for television, put Secretary of State George Shultz on the air following the film to discuss it. The irony of all this was that the damage shown in the film was modest compared to the probable destruction that would be wrought by current weapons.

Besides the nuclear weapons themselves, there is something frightening about the delivery systems—which now shorten the response time to minutes—and the defense warning systems. There have been enough glitches and false alarms to show that the missiles could be started on their way by mistake.

In the nuclear contest, the bombs keep getting bigger and the fuses shorter. But the superpower weapons and warning systems are not the only problems either.

Other countries have developed The Bomb or the capacity for making it. And on this proliferation of weapons, the Reagan administration, perhaps because of its single-minded focus on the U.S.S.R., also showed too little concern. In 1983, U.S. approval of some nuclear components to India, to South Africa and to Argentina (at the time still ruled by the military) did nothing to make the world a safer place. Greater cooperation between the two superpowers might at least control the spread of nuclear capabilities to other nations.

For many years, leaders of the U.S. and the U.S.S.R. said that there could be no victor in a nuclear war. Nikita Khrushchev said that in such a war "the living would envy the dead." By the spring of 1984, Ronald Reagan was also saying that nobody can win a

**ITEM: U.S. BOMBERS ALERTED ON COMPUTER'S FALSE
WARNING OF RUSSIAN MISSILE ATTACK**

*June 6, 1980*

nuclear war. But he said it only after negotiations with the Russians had come to a halt—and when he faced a re-election campaign in which diplomacy became politically more attractive.

During that campaign he reassured congressmen about his conciliatory attitude toward Russia, saying, "If they want to keep their Mickey Mouse system, that's okay."

Whatever Reagan's belated recognition of reality, it had to be dampened by a response he gave during a 1984 press conference. Asked about the nuclear arms race, he said, "They know they can't match us if there is such a race," and went on to tell how the Russians must come around or watch us gain superiority.

To many Americans there was indeed "such a race" and they were not hopeful about it.

In mid-April 1984, *U.S. News & World Report* published the results of a poll based on replies by 825 college students to a mail survey. In answer to the question "Do you expect a nuclear war in your lifetime?" 29.1 percent of the students said *yes* and 34.6 percent were unsure. In answer to the question "If you expect nuclear war, when do you think it will occur?" 50 percent responded: *Before the turn of the century.*

Only a few days before the results of this poll were published, author-editor Ronnie Duggar wrote a newspaper article about the several occasions when Ronald Reagan, as president, had spoken on the possibilities of Armageddon. One example was a taped conversation of October 1983, later published, in which the president said: "You know, I turn back to . . . the Old Testament and the signs foretelling Armageddon, and I find myself wondering if—if we're the generation that's going to see that come about. I don't know if you've noted any of those prophecies lately, but believe me, they certainly describe the times we're going through."

Tough, kids, but that's the way the planet crumbles.　　■

**"CHIEF, IF YOU COULD STAND A
LITTLE TO ONE SIDE—"**
*April 29, 1984*

**"IT SAYS HERE SOME OF THOSE
MIDDLE EAST COUNTRIES ARE
UNDER A CLOUD"**
*June 21, 1981*

**OLIVE BRANCHES**
*January 19, 1984*

**BABY BOOMS**
*May 31, 1981*

**CHARIOTS OF FIRE**
*April 20, 1982*

*January 8, 1984*

*May 20, 1984*

**"IT'S AMUSING THAT THEY THINK OF
THEMSELVES AS SUPERPOWERS"**
*November 29, 1981*

**"REMEMBER—ANY TIME YOU NEED JUST A *LITTLE* NUCLEAR WAR—"**

*August 11, 1981*

**"ABOUT SELLING OUR COMPUTER TECHNOLOGY TO RUSSIA—DON'T DO IT"**

*July 6, 1980*

**"DADDY HAS TO SUPPORT A HABIT"**

*April 3, 1983*

**"RIDDLE: HOW MANY MISSILES DOES IT TAKE TO PUT OUT ALL THE LIGHT BULBS?"**

*February 8, 1983*

May 27, 1984

**"BUT I'M ALREADY CLEANING UP"**
*November 23, 1980*

**ENVIRONMENT**
*March 11, 198.*

**"HE'LL BE IDEAL FOR WATCHING THE CHICKEN HOUSE—HE LOVES CHICKENS"**
*December 21, 1980*

**"LET US KNOW IF YOU HEAR ABOUT ANY CASES OF ENVIRONMENTAL PROTECTION"**
*March 11, 198.*

# A CAST OF CHARACTERS

Some things that keep happening for no good reason barely qualify as minor mysteries—like the way the dates on milk cartons at the local deli face the back of the refrigerator. I don't think anybody is trying to keep me from seeing the dates; the cartons just turn themselves that way. It's the same when you're driving and trucks pull alongside to pass just when you are approaching an important landmark you're looking for.

That's the kind of thing that happens at the end of a movie when I want to see who was who in the cast. All during the picture, a bunch of fellows have been scrunching down in the row ahead. But as soon as the movie ends and the credits begin to roll, these members of some local basketball team suddenly rise and stand as if at attention. As I try to see between them, they turn back and forth just enough to block out everything—until there rolls onto the screen the movie seal-of-approval, or whatever it is that concludes everything.

I stay for the cast and credits because I like to know who was who and who did what—even if it is, as they say, only a movie.

In the real-life theater of Washington, it is more important to know about the cast of an administration. That's because the president, who is the star, does his own casting and directing.

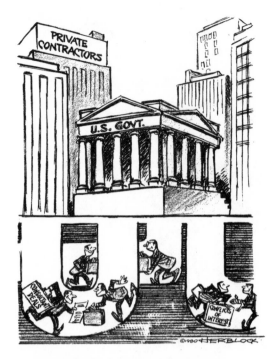

**OPERATION UNDERGROUND**
*July 8, 1980*

**"NO PROBLEM—IT'S AS GOOD AS IN"**
*January 14, 1981*

**"WELL, THEY SAID HE COULDN'T WITHDRAW"**
*June 4, 1981*

**"NEXT, WILL YOU WELCOME, PLEASE, ALEXANDER HAIG"**
*March 9, 1982*

President Reagan assembled one of the most unusual casts ever seen. Many of them not only played supporting roles but were also supported characters. The president supported them; and so did the taxpayers who paid the bills that they ran up.

If this cast were performing in a movie, it could be titled "Almost Anything Goes." It would not be X-rated, because that suggests sex, which has not figured prominently. The administration movie followed its own code, which might be called the New Morality. Under this code, cuddling up with a non-spouse is a no-no, but cuddling up with big-money interests is okay. And a little infidelity to the public trust is all right, too.

It probably rates an R because of violence to the general welfare. Or it could get an S for what has been described as Sleaze Factor or Scandal.

But first a short feature on past attractions.

Somebody in the Truman administration accepted a deep-freeze as a gift, which caused a hullabaloo that went on and on week after week.

One of President Eisenhower's close associates, Sherman Adams, accepted a carpet and a vicuna coat from a businessman, and the uproar was enormous. Despite Eisenhower's personal popularity and his plaintive cry that "I need him," he finally let Adams go.

President Carter's friend and close associate, Bert Lance, was budget director. But after long Senate hearings about his financial dealings as a banker before he entered the government, he eventually resigned.

At the time of the Bert Lance affair in the Carter administration, Ronald Reagan wrote: "What seemed to escape the president's notice . . . was the fact that the average citizen resents what seems to be undue special privilege for a few in high places."

In the Reagan administration, undue special privilege was certainly not for "a few in high places." It was for *many* in high places —along with sleaze, scandals and general ripoffs.

What Reagan directed was not a low-budget production. And there was nothing small about the cast except its ideals.

**"PERSONALLY, I'VE TRIED TO AVOID ACCEPTING ANYTHING BUT MONEY"**
*May 18, 1982*

**SCALE OF JUSTICE**
*April 19, 1984*

**"MAYBE IT DEPENDS ON WHICH BRANCH OF GOVERNMENT YOU'RE IN"**
*May 6, 1982*

**"I THINK WE GOT RID OF THAT CLOUD OVER DONOVAN'S OFFICE"**
*June 8, 1983*

Presented here is a partial cast, not necessarily in order of their appearance on the Washington set at the opening in January 1981.

For the part of Attorney General of the United States, Reagan selected William French Smith, whose previous role was that of Reagan's personal lawyer and a financial adviser.

Smith was selected to be attorney general in December 1980. On the last tax day of that year, December 31, Smith invested $16,500 in a tax shelter—on which he would later claim tax deductions of $66,000. Investors in this tax shelter were told that the Internal Revenue Service (IRS) would probably question deductions of that size for such an investment.

Less than two weeks later, the incoming attorney general left the Earl M. Jorgensen Co., where he served as a board member. The Jorgensen Co. gave Smith a farewell present—a $50,000 "severance payment"—its first ever made to a board member, and more money than Smith was paid in his six-year connection with the firm. Official precedent was against this kind of "severance payment" for one who was about to enter the government. But the man soon to become Attorney General of the United States either didn't know or didn't care. He took the money.

When these matters came to public attention, Smith decided to return the $50,000 and reduce his tax-shelter deduction to $16,500 —the amount actually invested. Yet he claimed there was no impropriety.

In March 1984, Smith was asked to reimburse the government about $11,000 after it was reported that his wife had misused a limousine for personal trips.

The attorney general is responsible for prosecuting tax evaders and for determining the appointment of special investigators in ethics cases.

William J. Casey, another Reagan friend, had a previous role as Reagan's presidential campaign manager in 1980. He was cast as director of the Central Intelligence Agency (CIA). Casey did not put his financial holdings in a blind trust—the usual procedure for officials in high level positions. He continued active trading in stocks.

In 1981, while head of a government agency dealing in worldwide

"SIR, ABOUT YOUR CHOICE OF MR. HUGEL AS CHIEF OF SECRET OPERATIONS—"

*July 15, 1981*

"WE HAVE COMPLETE CONFIDENCE IN WHAT'S-HIS-NAME HERE"

*July 17, 1981*

"WHAT TESTIMONIALS! WHAT HIGH STANDARDS OF PUBLIC SERVICE!"

*December 3, 1981*

"THIS IS THE HOT LINE—IT'S TO HIS STOCK BROKER"

*June 3, 1983*

intelligence, he sold more than $600,000 in oil stocks before world oil prices dropped. In 1982 his tradings came to $3 million. He finally put his holdings in a blind trust in July 1983, only after the Senate threatened to pass a resolution requiring this. There were also omissions in Casey's financial disclosure statement that later had to be corrected.

A 1981 Senate investigating committee had reported on Casey, in something less than an accolade, that he was not "unfit to serve" in office. At least one committee member said that this not-unfavorable decision was arrived at with a great deal of non-enthusiasm.

Casey brought into the administration cast another interesting character: Max Hugel, also a 1980 campaign operative, who said he had known Casey for about 20 years. He made Hugel deputy CIA director for clandestine operations, a highly sensitive post, even though Hugel lacked experience in intelligence, in government and in foreign affairs. When two brothers, former business associates of Hugel, accused Hugel of shady stock dealings, he denied the charges. But he resigned the same day the charges were published.

After the Hugel matter came to public attention, Casey dropped out of sight temporarily, and I drew him with a bag over his head. This continued to seem appropriate for the man who was often buttoning up his overt–covert activities or drawing a blank on what happened—so I left the bag on him.

When Casey surfaced again, he said he had known Hugel for only about 17 months. But at the time he appointed Hugel, he said they had a long and trusting relationship.

Casey and his many activities never stayed out of the news for long. In mid-1984 the IRS was cross-examining him about claimed deductions. In one instance he had, over a period of four years, taken deductions of about $60,000 on an investment of $95.

Another early member of the Reagan cast was Richard V. Allen, assistant to the president for national security affairs. Allen received ten $100 bills and three watches from Japanese newsmen. The money, he said, was intended as an inappropriate gift for First Lady Nancy Reagan. He intercepted it, put it in a safe and forgot it. He resigned his position.

**"HOW WOULD HE NOTICE THOSE PAPERS IF THEY WEREN'T RECEIPTS FROM A STOCK BROKER?"**

*July 7, 1983*

**"IF WE HURRY HIM OUT, NOBODY WILL NOTICE"**

*March 18, 1983*

**"SOMETHING WRONG WITH OUR RECIPES?"**

*August 10, 1983*

**"WHAT TRUNK? WHAT CAR?"**

*June 16, 1982*

Thomas C. Reed was deputy assistant to the president for national security. The Securities and Exchange Commission said that he made $427,000 in profits on an investment of $3,125 based on inside information. He gave up the $427,000.

Secretary of Labor Raymond J. Donovan had been executive vice president of the Schiavone Construction Co. in New Jersey before appointment to the Reagan Cabinet. In 1982 a special prosecutor investigated allegations against Donovan involving union corruption and ties with organized crime figures. The special prosecutor concluded that there was "insufficient credible evidence" to support any criminal charges.

In March 1983, two former labor union officials were indicted on charges of conspiring to impede the Donovan investigation.

William V. Shannon, in *The Boston Globe* May 23, 1984, wrote that "a federal prosecutor in Brooklyn is investigating the deaths of two underworld figures. . . . Both men were prospective witnesses in the Donovan inquiry, and both were murdered while it was under way."

Whatever Donovan's connections in the construction business, as Secretary of Labor he had little contact with the AFL-CIO, the largest association of unions in the country.

Mary Thornton and Howard Kurtz of *The Washington Post* disclosed information on an entire group of cast members including deputy Secretary of Defense Paul Thayer.

The Securities and Exchange Commission charged that Thayer leaked inside stock information while serving on the boards of three corporations. He resigned to fight the charges.

Leslie Lenkowsky, nominated to be deputy director of the U.S. Information Agency, was accused in a congressional staff report of lying to Congress about responsibility for a "blacklist" of people—mostly liberals and Democrats—barred from speaking abroad for the USIA. On May 15, 1984, he became the first Reagan nominee to be rejected outright by a Senate committee.

Kurtz wrote an article about Frederick Andre, a member of the Interstate Commerce Commission. Andre said that kickbacks in the trucking industry should be viewed as just "discounts or rebates." He

**"POST-WATERGATE MORALITY"**
*June 20, 1982*

saw nothing wrong with convicted felons running a trucking industry from prison. He said the commission should not worry about bribes because they are "one of the clearest instances of the free market at work."

In the Reagan cast there have been any number of characters who have played smaller roles but who have known how to run up big bills. To break the tedium of high-level sleaze and scandals, here are a couple of lighter notes:

Another *Washington Post* story gave some interesting information on free marketer Bill J. Sloan, a regional director of Housing and Urban Development. Sloan was forced to pay back $6,800 he charged the government for private travel and meals. Explaining his charge of $1,026 for meals while living at home, he said that he generally ate in restaurants because "my wife doesn't like to cook."

Sloan also said he preferred driving his own car "because you are only allowed to drive a government vehicle 55 miles an hour and I like to drive faster." His bills for travel expenses ran faster too.

Kurtz also brightened the lives of readers with the classic case of Emanuel S. Savas, former assistant Housing and Urban Development secretary for policy development, who used staff members in his office to type and proofread his book. The title: *Privatizing the Public Sector.*

Former deputy Secretary of Transportation Darrell M. Trent said, in explaining $3,219 for a first class Paris ticket, that coach class would not have enabled him to reach his destination on time. Trent acknowledged that both sections were on the same plane. Well, maybe the first class section was a few yards ahead of the coach section.

A person who believed as strongly as President Reagan did in private initiative could hardly fault many of his appointees who showed enterprise in using public funds. As far as the rest of us were concerned, the only trouble was that the private initiatives of these public "servants" came at our expense.

Did you ever hear of Dennis E. LeBlanc? He was a close Reagan associate—a former highway patrolman who served on the security detail when Reagan was governor of California and later worked on

"THE NOVEL THING ABOUT TURNING
OVER THE WEATHER SERVICE IS
THAT IT WOULD BE DONE
OFFICIALLY"

*March 15, 1983*

WHILE THE CAT'S AWAY

*January 2, 1983*

"THE ARROGANCE OF CONGRESSMEN
AND PUBLIC RIFFRAFF WANTING AN
ACCOUNTING FROM *ME!*"

*January 5, 1982*

SHELTER

*May 27, 1982*

Reagan's ranch in California. He was appointed an "associate administrator for policy analysis and development" in a branch of the Commerce Department. But he did not spend much time in Washington. A lot of his time was devoted to chopping wood, building fences and doing chores at the Reagan ranch. The pay: $58,500 a year.

Reagan was never one to tolerate public welfare people. When Reagan was at the ranch, he could *see* his friend LeBlanc working.

Nancy Harvey Steorts had her government office renovated at a cost of $10,000. She also wanted the driver of her car to wear a uniform, and threatened to fire the man when he said he couldn't afford one. Some friends chipped in to buy the driver a suit. Mrs. Steorts's position: chairman of the Consumer Product Safety Commission. What consumer doesn't want to know what kind of curtains and decorations you can get for an office for $10,000 and how safe they are? What consumer doesn't want her chauffeur dressed in a good safe uniform?

Mrs. Steorts was rather frugal compared to Robert P. Nimmo, who was appointed by Reagan to run the Veterans Administration. He spent $54,183 redecorating *his* office. But he wasn't as extravagant as you might think either. He sent the old furniture to his daughter, a public affairs office director in the Commerce Department. Nimmo resigned shortly before the General Accounting Office (GAO) released a report critical of his travel and other expenses.

Secretary of the Treasury Donald T. Regan is one of the administration officials who has to spend $300 to $464 a day for hotel accommodations when he travels. But who would want people to get the impression that the U.S. Treasury was short of money?

Onward to other members of the cast:

Charles Z. Wick, head of the U.S. Information Agency (USIA) installed, at taxpayers' expense, a $32,000 security system at his house in Washington. He repaid $22,000 of the cost on advice of White House counsel.

But Wick is best known for his telephone conversations—specifically his recording of them without notifying parties at the other end of the phone. He did this taping despite a warning from the USIA

**VOICES OF AMERICA**

*January 6, 1984*

**"NOT TO WORRY—IT'S JUST THAT WE'VE BEEN HIRING SOME STUPID IDEOLOGUES AROUND HERE"**

*February 16, 1984*

**"MAYBE HE SHOULD BE CITED FOR CONTEMPT OF PUBLIC INTELLIGENCE"**

*March 7, 1982*

**"THOSE ARE MY KIND OF BEACH BOYS"**

*April 14, 1983*

general counsel that it would be illegal. In January 1984, he issued a statement apologizing for his surreptitious tapings.

Wick always seemed to have trouble with telephones even before the breakup of the Bell system.

He had phones in his house installed at public expense. When the GAO discovered the phone charges, and federal auditors ruled the use of the phones illegal, Wick repaid $4,436 for personal calls and service charges on the phones. That was in June 1984, half a year after he apologized for his tapings.

Secretary of the Interior James G. Watt may be best remembered for statements he made. One was the announcement of his selection for the 1983 Fourth-of-July entertainment in Washington and his reference to rock groups attracting "the wrong element." Another was the reference to the people he appointed to a commission: "a black, . . . a woman, two Jews, and a cripple." Shortly after this, he resigned.

He deserves more mention than that.

In April 1983, the U.S. Park Police disclosed that the Interior Department was spending more than $300,000 a year on nine body-guards to protect Secretary Watt from threats on his life. The nine bodyguards "travel all over the country with him to guard him" said the Park Police.

In an interview at that time about a Holocaust memorial museum, Watt said that he and his wife supported the idea and were sensitive to the subject because they themselves were "persecuted evangelical Christians."

In December 1981, the "persecuted" Watt had used the Custis-Lee Mansion in Arlington National Cemetery for a breakfast party and a cocktail party which may have violated the National Park Service guidelines. The GAO found that Watt left an unpaid bill for $6,517.30. Watt refused to pay, and the tab was eventually picked up by the Republican National Committee.

Investigations by a congressional committee and by the GAO showed that in 1982, Watt had often used a $1.5 million plane dispatched long distances to pick up Watt and sometimes his relatives.

"I JUST DON'T KNOW IF OIL LEASES
ARE MY BAG"

*July 30, 1981*

"MAKE IT FAST—WE DON'T HAVE ALL
THE TIME IN THE WORLD"

*January 20, 1983*

"WHAT A COINCIDENCE—WE JUST
HAPPEN TO HAVE DESIGNED A
PARCEL THAT JUST HAPPENS TO FIT
YOUR PORTFOLIO"

*June 12, 1983*

"IT WOULDN'T BE WHOLESOME TO
HAVE THE WRONG ELEMENT
DRINKING OVER THERE"

*April 7, 1983*

He also used it to make political fund-raising appearances.

GAO investigators found that in 1981, in a period of about four months, Watt spent about $69,000 of department funds traveling on the special plane and that $39,000 was written off as fire-fighting expenses.

Although Watt had ordered strict curbs on Interior Department non-essential travel, he tried to abolish an office within the department that had kept tabs on airplane use.

Before becoming a member of the Reagan administration, Watt was an attorney for the Mountain States Legal Foundation, representing energy companies that wanted more control over federal lands and resources. As Secretary of the Interior, he was in a position to turn over to private interests as much control over federal resources as he could, as fast as he could.

He put in place a program to offer leases to practically all the U.S. coastal waters for offshore drilling by 1987. He drafted plans to lease oil shale and tar sands in the Rocky Mountain states in 1984. And he put all geothermal steam resources on the market. Despite the fact that Watt was not Secretary of Energy and that oil costs had dropped, he cited energy needs as the excuse for leasing public lands and the U.S. coastline.

Even congressmen inured to administration give-away, lease-away policies were shocked by the crassness of the Interior Department coal leasing operations.

An investigation ordered by the House Appropriations Committee spent eight months working on a report issued in April 1983. It concluded that Watt had leased government coal reserves to private companies at "fire sale" prices producing "windfall profits."

The report also disclosed that more than a month before an auction of a billion tons of government coal in 1982, confidential Interior Department data was leaked to the coal industry. This leak, which even some officials within the department called "scandalous," was connected to the biggest auction of coal development rights in U.S. history.

In May 1983, the GAO gave results of its own investigation. It found that the coal rights had been leased for $100 million less than

REAGAN ADMINISTRATION OIL AND COAL LEASES

HARDING ADMINISTRATION TEAPOT DOME LEASE

©1983 HERBLOCK

"PIKER!"

May 13, 1983

they were worth, despite a federal law requiring the government to get a fair price for its resources. The GAO mentioned the same inside information leaks and the undervaluing of leased resources that the House committee did. But it also noted something else: Some of the tracts offered for leasing were "custom-fitted" to be attractive to only one company.

Fortunately for Watt, and for Reagan, too, Watt's loose-lip words drew more attention than his deeds in support of administration policy.

Scandal was more easily recognized in the Environmental Protection Agency (EPA) under administrator Anne Burford (formerly Anne Gorsuch).

Rep. Morris Udall (D-Ariz.) said that Watt and Burford "have done for the environment what Bonnie and Clyde did for banks."

The EPA, charged with cleaning the environment, required so much cleaning up itself that more than a dozen of its higher officials eventually were forced to resign.

The EPA was supposed to report violations of its regulations to the Justice Department. But as early as November 1981, it had become obvious that the EPA was reporting fewer than before. Spokesmen said that Burford preferred to rely on voluntary compliance.

In early 1982 she told Congress that environmentalists were greatly exaggerating the adverse effect of proposed changes in federal air quality controls on national parks and recreational areas. She explained that the changes in regulations would only double the pollution levels.

Petroleum and refining companies disliked standards for reducing poisonous lead in gasoline; and Burford planned to relax these standards. She let Thriftway refining company know that it would not be prosecuted for violating a current EPA regulation.

Even with the creation of a $1.6 billion Superfund for cleaning up hazardous waste dumps, the EPA did little cleanup work. When a congressional committee investigated, one EPA official said that cleanup of certain dumps was postponed for political reasons until after the 1982 general elections.

**"LOOK—I'M A CONSERVATIONIST
NOW"**

*July 8, 1983*

*July 23, 1982*

**DARKEST INTERIOR**

*May 1, 1983*

**"AND I'VE GOT A FUNNY BLACKFACE
ROUTINE FOR YOU"**

*September 22, 1983*

The Reagan administration withheld subpoenaed documents on hazardous waste cleanups, claiming executive privilege, and in December 1982, Burford was cited for contempt by the House of Representatives.

Rita Lavelle headed EPA's office of Solid Waste and Emergency Response, which had responsibility for the Superfund. She was fired by President Reagan on Feb. 7, 1983.

Testimony in congressional hearings disclosed that two shredding machines were brought into that EPA office on Jan. 6 and were taken out on Feb. 10. In mid February, a congressional investigator charged that an EPA official attempted to remove 15 boxes of documents from the agency.

Despite the paper shredding, and the charges of sweetheart deals and conflicts of interest, the only EPA official convicted was Lavelle. She was cited for perjury and sentenced to jail.

Burford resigned under fire in March 1983. But deputy EPA director John W. Hernandez did not succeed her. Members of his staff said he had allowed Dow Chemical Co. to edit a critical EPA report on Dow's part in dioxin contamination.

Burford was back in the news the following year. On July 2, 1984, President Reagan appointed her to another position—chairman of the National Advisory Committee on Oceans and Atmosphere. One of the functions of this committee is to make recommendations on offshore dumping. The announcement of the appointment came just before a White House luncheon to which Reagan had invited a group of conservative environmentalists for some election-year fence mending. This put a firecracker in the peace pipe. The conservationists, at first stunned by the news, expressed outrage. As far as political rapprochement was concerned, the luncheon was a shambles.

At a July 24, 1984 news conference, Reagan renewed his expressions of satisfaction with Burford. Despite a request by the Republican-controlled Senate that he withdraw her name, Reagan said he would not do so.

Burford described her appointment to the committee as a "nothingburger" and she soon withdrew.

**"IT'S JUST A MODIFIED LIMITED STONE WALL"**

*March 4, 1983*

**"HOW COULD ANYONE THINK WE HAVE SOMETHING TO HIDE?"**

*February 18, 1983*

**"WE'D LIKE TO SEND IN AN INTERNATIONAL RED CROSS INSPECTION TEAM"**

*February 4, 1982*

**" . . . THAT I WILL FAITHFULLY EXECUTE THE OFFICE . . . "**

*February 24, 1983*

We come now to a principal supporting—and supported—character, Edwin Meese III. Meese was a legal secretary and adviser to Gov. Reagan in California, and played a leading role in the 1980 presidential campaign before he moved to Washington as a special adviser to the president. In 1984, when William French Smith decided to resign as attorney general, Reagan chose Meese to succeed him. The nomination to this post, which requires Senate confirmation, was the beginning of Meese's political problems. His financial problems began before that.

He had a house in La Mesa, California that had been on the market for 20 months; and the subsequent sale developed into a house-that-Jack-built scenario.

This was the house that Meese sold.

Thomas Barrack arranged the sale of the house that Meese sold.

Irv Howard bought the house when Barrack arranged the disposition of the house that Meese sold.

Fifty thousand dollars was the estimated loss that Howard took in reselling the house that Meese sold.

Great American Savings and Loan Association arranged friendly terms for a man it didn't know named Howard, who bought and resold at a loss the house that Meese sold.

Barrack, who arranged the sale, made a $70,000 loan to one of the buyers and later forgave the loan, to expedite the purchase of the house that Meese sold.

Who were all these kind, generous people and what happened to them?

President Reagan named Barrack an assistant secretary in the Interior Department.

John McKean, Meese's tax accountant, who arranged loans to Meese totaling $60,000, was later appointed to the U.S. Postal Service Board of Governors. McKean said he understood Meese and White House deputy chief of staff Michael Deaver had submitted his name for the post. Previously McKean had also arranged a $58,000 loan for Deaver to enable him to take part in a tax shelter.

Meese at one time owed Great American $420,000, but the bank

**"WE WERE JUST MAKING CONFETTI
TO CELEBRATE TEN YEARS SINCE
WATERGATE"**

*February 13, 1983*

**"FUNDS ARE FUNDS—ANYONE COULD
GET MIXED UP"**

*March 23, 1983*

**"WE CONSIDER IT CLOSED"**

*September 29, 1983*

**"NO NEED TO CALL THE POLICE—
EVERYTHING LOOKS ALL RIGHT
HERE"**

*August 12, 1983*

continued lending him money even after he was 15 months behind in loan payments.

Chairman of Great American was Gordon Luce, fund-raiser and an appointee of Gov. Reagan in California. President Reagan named him an alternate U.S. delegate to the United Nations.

Another officer of Great American was Edwin Gray, Gov. Reagan's press secretary in California; he was later named by President Reagan to be head of the Federal Home Loan Bank Board (where he renovated his office at a cost of $47,000).

Then it developed that Meese's wife Ursula had received a personal interest free loan of $15,000 that Meese had "inadvertently failed" to list in his disclosure statement to the Office of Government Ethics.

Edwin Thomas, who made the loan, was later named Meese's deputy at the White House.

In March 1984, Meese had another apparent memory failure. He had been chief of staff in the Reagan 1980 campaign but could not recall memos about efforts to obtain strategy papers from the Carter campaign. Nor could he recall Carter documents that had been sent to him.

At Meese's Senate hearings a staff member counted 79 times on a whole range of issues when Meese had said he couldn't recall.

Later that month a special prosecutor was named to investigate Meese's affairs. Along with the finances and the briefing-paper incidents, the investigation would include possible violation of federal law against selling government jobs, possible trading law violations in connection with a stock purchase, and Meese's promotion in the Army reserves. An Army inspector general's report showed that Meese had been improperly transferred from retired to reserve status and had then been promoted to colonel.

His nomination to be Attorney General of the United States was put on hold, and William French Smith continued in the post.

Smith also continued doing something else—he continued showing a remarkable lack of enthusiasm for an independent investigation

**DUMP**
*February 10, 1983*

**"WE'VE GIVEN IT TWO OF OUR FAIREST MAIDENS"**
*March 11, 1983*

**"TOO BAD, BERT—YOU CAME TO WASHINGTON JUST A FEW YEARS TOO SOON"**

*March 8, 1984*

**"SIR, DO YOU DARE TO IMPLY THAT MY CONDUCT MIGHT BE ANYTHING LESS THAN IMPECCABLE?"**

*March 20, 1984*

**"SOMEBODY MINED THE I.R.S. OFFICES!"**

*May 16, 1984*

**"FOLLOWING THE EXAMPLE OF EDWIN MEESE, I INSIST ON A THOROUGH INVESTIGATION"**

*March 25, 1984*

of "Debategate"—the appearance of the Carter campaign papers in the 1980 Reagan camp.

Presidential aide James A. Baker III recalled having received such papers from campaign manager William J. Casey. But Casey couldn't recall anything about them.

It might have seemed simple enough for a president who wanted to get to the bottom of the matter, as Reagan put it, to do so. But he didn't.

Reagan started out by saying that it was "much ado about nothing." After pooh-poohing the matter and trying to kick it away, he finally turned it over to his friend and former lawyer, Attorney General William French Smith.

On Feb. 23, 1984, after what was said to be an eight-month investigation, the Justice Department issued a brief report saying that there was no credible evidence of any criminal behavior.

Casey couldn't remember anything. Meese couldn't remember anything. It recalled Sen. Sam Ervin's words at a Watergate hearing when he referred to a witness having a "forgettory."

Bob Woodward, writing in *The Washington Post*, pointed out that here were many examples of inside information on the Carter campaign. Here were memos specifically addressed to these principals: "from reliable White House mole," said one; "our White House source," another was labeled.

A memo dated Sept. 12, 1980, sent to Meese from a Reagan campaign aide, said that campaign manager Casey "wants more information from the Carter camp and wants it circulated."

Woodward was impressed by the number of people the FBI did *not* interview—including several top people in the Carter and Reagan campaigns. He also found that Smith and FBI director William Webster consulted regularly on the FBI investigation. One of the matters they discussed was the fact that Theodore M. Gardner, the special agent in charge of the Washington field office, had talked to Woodward:

He confirmed information I had from others that the FBI wanted to give lie detector tests to some senior Reagan adminis-

"THE OFFICIAL ANSWERS ARE: (A)
WHAT? (B) WHO, ME? AND (C) HOW'S
THAT AGAIN?"

*June 26, 1983*

"CALL NIXON AND FIND OUT IF THAT
JUDGE CAN MAKE US OBEY THE
LAW"

*May 17, 1984*

"THE GREAT THING ABOUT THIS
PLACE IS YOU DON'T GET MANY
QUESTIONS ABOUT THE CARTER
PAPERS"

*August 4, 1983*

"JIMMY WHO?"

*March 9, 1984*

tration officials, including White House Chief of Staff Baker and CIA Director Casey. It is normal FBI policy that the head of each field office has discretion in how to deal with the press. Gardner evidently felt the conversation was proper; he recorded it in his office log.

Special agent Gardner was transferred out of town.

The Justice Department and the FBI, according to Woodward, also suffered memory lapses. They couldn't remember seeing anything like a memo dated August 11, 1980, which Max Hugel had routed through to Meese. It said, "Bill Casey asked me to have you review this memo which fell into my hands and to come up with some of our own strategy on this particular subject that might counteract this effort." The memo was attached to a Carter campaign memo on farm and rural strategy.

The memo had been in the Justice Department files and was obtained by a House subcommittee investigating "Debategate."

**"WE DO ALL THE DIGGING WE CAN"**
*February 26, 1984*      189

THE BRIEFING-PAPERS CASE

HANG IN THERE TILL ELECTION DAY!

Ronald (WE-WANT-TO-GET TO THE BOTTOM OF THIS) Reagan

Edwin (WHO-ME?) Meese

Wm French (STONEWALL) Smith

Wm J. (I CAN'T REMEMBER) Casey

©1984 HERBLOCK

*May 24, 1984*

After an 11-month investigation, the House subcommittee, under Rep. Donald Albosta (D-Mich.), issued a lengthy report that showed a greater effort to get at the facts than the administration inquiry.

It said the "better evidence" showed that Casey was the conduit for entry of the "Carter debate briefing materials" into the Reagan campaign. It also cited testimony bearing out Baker's recollection. Margaret Tutwiler, a longtime aide to Baker, said that he had told her about receiving the papers from Casey.

The committee urged the attorney general to appoint a special prosecutor.

In early March 1984, U.S. District Court Judge Harold H. Greene ruled that the Justice Department "appears to have simply ignored" the requirements of the Ethics in Government Act, which were to "establish procedures for the avoidance of the actual or perceived conflicts of interest that may arise when the attorney general investigates alleged criminal wrongdoing by other high government officials." Greene called for a special prosecutor.

William French Smith hastened to appeal Greene's ruling and won a reversal.

In a June 1984 televised news conference, Reagan asserted that "no one" in his 1980 campaign saw a Carter briefing book. Speaking about the papers that were uncovered, he said "all of it had been out in the open and made public . . . before the debate."

But the Albosta subcommittee reported:

> Before the Oct. 28, 1980 debate between President Carter and Governor Reagan, the Reagan-Bush campaign obtained foreign policy and national defense briefing papers prepared to assist President Carter in that debate, and also acquired briefing papers on those subjects prepared for Vice President Mondale.
>
> The Carter debate briefing papers were used by persons connected with the Reagan-Bush campaign to enhance Governor Reagan's performance in the debate. The persons using these papers were aware that they were using Carter debate briefing materials.

The report also said that former Reagan campaign aides David R. Gergen and Frank Hodsoll "each produced from their files copies of the Carter foreign policy 'big book' . . .," and that other campaign aides remember seeing a more condensed briefing book on foreign policy prepared only a week before the Cleveland debate.

There is a popular notion that since Watergate the standards of government morality have become terribly strict. We now have legislation like the Ethics in Government Act—which Attorney General Smith chose to interpret in his own way.

Actually, the Watergate scandals succeeded in numbing public views of morality to a point where anything less than the expected impeachment of a president for criminal activities failed to arouse outrage.

The worst form of corruption is acceptance of corruption.

Writers dealing with the subject of Reagan administration misconduct nearly always add that "this is not Watergate."

It doesn't *need* to be a Watergate. Dishonesty is dishonesty. Scandals are scandals. Corruption is corruption. The Reagan administration contained all of them and over a far wider area than previous administrations.

The fact that public officials can stay out of jail is not enough to warrant keeping them in public office.

We now return to the cast. Such a remarkable collection couldn't have been assembled by accident. The White House director and his cast members obviously have had an affinity for each other. There are many more who deserve mention.

Let the credits and the discredits roll.

From The *National Journal* of Jan. 17, 1984:

**William M. Bell,** who was Reagan's choice to be full-time chairman of the Equal Employment Opportunity Commission, was president of a Detroit job recruiting firm that had not placed any employees in at least a year and had never been listed in either the white or yellow pages of the phone book. His nomination was withdrawn in February 1982.

When **Donald P. Bogard** was hired as president of the Legal Services Corp. at the urging of board chairman William F. Harvey, he negotiated a contract—since downgraded by Congress—that paid for his membership in a private club and guaranteed him a full year's severance pay.

**Charles M. Butler III,** Federal Energy Regulatory Commission chairman, agreed to excuse himself from considering appeals of cases involving clients he or associates at his Houston law firm represented before the commission's predecessor, the Federal Power Commission. But he said he would not disqualify himself from deciding new cases involving his former clients.

Anne Burford's husband, **Robert F. Burford,** the Interior Department's Bureau of Land Management director, owns a 25 percent interest in a family cattle and sheep ranch that has permits to graze on 33,614 acres of bureau lands. Burford obtained a waiver of provisions that prohibited him from holding an interest in land administered by the bureau by selling his grazing permits and cattle to a limited partnership set up by his three sons who own the ranch with him.

**Carlos C. Campbell,** former assistant Commerce secretary for economic development, resigned while under fire for providing grants to firms with questionable credentials, some of them run by personal friends.

Presidential scheduler **Joseph W. Canzeri** resigned following disclosure that he had billed both the Republican National Committee and the government for personal expenses and that he had received loans of $200,000 each from Laurance S. Rockefeller and Newport Beach (Calif.) realtor Donald M. Koll at favorable rates to buy a home in Washington.

**Michael Cardenas,** administrator of the Small Business Administration, was forced out following investigations of SBA grants, including one to an Albuquerque (N.M.) contractor who was under criminal investigation.

**John B. Crowell Jr.,** assistant Agriculture secretary for natural resources and environment, was general counsel of Louisiana-Pacific Corp. from 1973–1981.

He developed the strategy for a subsidiary, Ketchikan Pulp Co., to circumvent provisions of the small-business set-aside program that he now administers. Crowell failed to include on his personal financial disclosure statement his job as assistant secretary of Ketchikan Pulp, which was convicted of antitrust violations.

Deputy White House chief of staff **Michael K. Deaver** wrote a diet book that could earn him well over the statutory annual limit on outside earnings (15 percent of salary). He avoided the limit by contracting to be paid only 15 percent a year while in office.

Former Deputy Commerce Secretary **Guy M. Fiske** was negotiating for a job at the Communications Satellite Corp. while he was supposed to be in charge of negotiations for sale of the department's weather satellites to the company.

While chairman of the Indiana Senate's Natural Resources Committee, **James R. Harris** (now director of the Interior Department's Office of Surface Mining) negotiated a real estate deal with the chief Indiana lobbyist for the coal company Amax Inc. to buy land at favorable prices.

**B. Sam Hart,** Reagan's first nominee to the Civil Rights Commission, was in default on a $100,000 Small Business Administration loan. Two weeks after his nomination, the SBA agreed to refinance the loan. Hart was also delinquent on repaying a $200,000 loan from the Pennsylvania Minority Business Development Authority and owed $4,400 in back taxes. He asked that his nomination be withdrawn.

**Arthur Hull Hayes Jr.,** former commissioner of the Food and Drug Administration, billed the government for some trips that were paid for by businesses and trade organizations. Hayes accepted speaking fees and free lodging from private groups with interests before the FDA, in addition to travel expenses.

Federal Aviation Administration chief, **J. Lynn Helms** resigned after being accused of having operated a business that took over small companies and bled them dry of funds.

**Donald I. Hovde,** former Housing and Urban Development undersecretary, paid back $3,100 to cover the cost of a government chauffeur he used to commute to work.

**Ernest W. Lefever's** nomination to be assistant secretary of State for human rights and humanitarian affairs was in trouble even before it was revealed that his Ethics and Public Policy Center had received a $25,000 research grant from Nestle Corp. prior to issuing an exculpatory report on international marketing of Nestle's infant formula. That iced it, and Lefever withdrew his nomination.

On the financial disclosure statement filed when he joined the Administration, Navy Secretary **John Lehman** said he had reorganized his consulting firm, Abington Corp., as a personal holding company. Records he filed with the District of Columbia corporate records office contradicted that statement.

When **James L. Malone** was confirmed to be assistant secretary of State for oceans and international, environmental and scientific affairs, he promised not to get involved in issues concerning his former clients, including the Taiwan Power Co. But the Senate Foreign Relations Committee determined that he violated his promise by lobbying for an Export-Import Bank loan to the power company.

The Federal Trade Commission has been sued by the National Center for Auto Safety on the ground that commission chairman **James C. Miller III** who received $75,000 in consulting fees from General Motors Corp. from 1978–1980, should not have participated in the commission's settlement of a GM auto-defects case.

The nomination of **James W. Sanderson** to be assistant EPA administrator for policy and resource management was withheld after it was disclosed that Sanderson represented organizations regulated by EPA at the same time that he was being paid by the agency as a consultant.

**Norman B. Ture,** former undersecretary of the Treasury for tax and economic affairs, urged the department to purchase an economic model from an accounting firm that was in the process of buying the rights to the model from him.

## From *The New Republic* of April 16, 1984:

**Gerald Carmen,** General Services Administration—failed to list a $425,000 low-interest government loan on a financial disclosure form; allegedly placed family members and friends in government jobs.

**Michael J. Connolly,** general counsel, Equal Employment Opportunity Commission—resigned amid allegations he conspired to end an EEOC investigation of a company represented by his brother.

**Robert Funkhouser,** EPA director of international activities—resigned after allegations that he helped the Dow Chemical Company influence trade talks on toxic chemicals.

**William Harvey,** chairman of Legal Services Corporation—collected $25,000 in consulting fees from the government over an eleven-month period.

**William S. Heffelfinger,** assistant Secretary of Energy—accused of falsifying his resume, deceiving federal investigators, and violating civil service merit protection regulations.

**William E. McCann,** ambassador to Ireland—nomination withdrawn after allegations he was involved in shady business deals and had connections to organized crime.

**John McElderry,** Denver regional administrator, Department of Health and Human Services—resigned after allegations he used his federal position to promote and sell Amway products.

**William Olsen,** board member of the Legal Services Corporation—collected $19,721 in consulting fees in 1982.

**Richard N. Perle,** Assistant Secretary of Defense—urged the Secretary of the Army in 1982 to buy weapons from an Israeli firm that had paid him $50,000 in consulting fees prior to his joining the government.

**Armand Reiser,** counselor to the Department of Energy—resigned after disclosures he failed to reveal $106,000 in earnings from five energy-related companies.

## From *The Washington Post* of May 30, 1984:

**Louis J. Cordia** of the EPA's office of federal activities, who resigned after the agency confirmed that he had compiled a blacklist of employees and consultants to be denied promotions because of their political views.

**John Horton,** an assistant administrator of the EPA, and **Matthew N. Novick,** the EPA's inspector general, who both were charged with making government employees work on their private business on government time. Both denied wrongdoing but were ordered by the White House to resign.

**Robert M. Perry,** the agency's general counsel, who resigned after reports that he participated in the settlement of a hazardous-waste complaint against a subsidiary of his former employer, Exxon. Perry said that he left government for personal reasons.

**Isidoro Rodriguez,** former head of minority affairs at the Agriculture Department, who was reported to have collected unemployment benefits while working as a consultant before receiving his federal appointment. He was dismissed from government because of a controversial memo he wrote on civil-rights policy.

**Wayne W. Tangye,** Sloan's deputy, who had $12,000 in expense vouchers questioned by government investigators. Tangye resigned without making restitution; the government attached his last paycheck and his pension.

**Victor M. Thompson Jr.,** president of the Synthetic Fuels Corp., who resigned after an internal report said he violated ethics rules by voting on decisions involving government funds for a Texas oilman whose help he had sought to shore up his private business. Thompson said his votes were not influenced by his private affairs.

195

And finally from an Associated Press article on William J. Casey dated July 22, 1981:

A plagiarism suit brought by Harry Fields in 1959 contend-[ed] that a tax booklet edited by Casey had used, without authorization, 2½ pages of a manuscript that Fields had written on employee benefit plans.

According to court records, Fields gave Casey the manuscript to relay it to a New York publishing house, but Casey first showed it to one of his assistants who was editing an article for Casey's tax booklet on the same subject. Casey said he was unaware the assistant had copied the manuscript and used a portion of it in the booklet.

A jury awarded Fields damages of $40,425, including $12,850 in punitive damages from Casey. Subsequently, Fields agreed to accept an immediate payment of $20,500 and to allow the verdict to be expunged from the record and to have the transcript sealed.

In 1971, Casey told the Senate Banking Committee the settlement came about after the case judge, J. Braxton Craven, told attorneys that the verdict was not supported by evidence and that he intended to set it aside.

However, when Judge Craven was asked about Casey's claim, he denied making such a statement and told the committee that on the contrary, he felt the jury's verdict was "amply" supported by the evidence.    ■

# AROUND THE WORLD
# IN 80 SECONDS

A long time ago, before movie houses grew in clusters and before everyone had been everywhere, there were short films called travelogues.

They showed parts of the world you wouldn't otherwise see. There was a running commentary about the charming natives and their quaint customs. And as the sunset silhouetted the village temples, the commentator would bid a reluctant goodbye to lovely Kashmir, Tahiti or Pago Pago.

Today we see things all over the world on television, live by satellite. Much of it is not charming but violent. Somebody in a show once said, "We don't go to the theater to see violence, rape and incest —we get enough of that at home."

These days we get lots of violence at home *and* at the movies.

Without benefit of satellite, here is a brief travelogue of places where there are still customs that are quaint, though not always charming.

We can begin with one of the quaintest of all, a unique place called South Africa. Here a large group of civilized black people is ruled by a small group of primitive white tribesmen. We would be happy to see the government of South Africa sink with the setting sun.

**"ROOT THEM OUT AND DRIVE THEM AWAY—THEY OBVIOUSLY BELONG TO SOME STRANGE TRIBE"**
*November 29, 1983*

*April 20, 1984*

**"GENTLEMEN! GENTLEMEN!"**
*January 26, 1983*

**"THE OUTFITS ARE FROM KING HUSSEIN—HE SENDS THEM TO EVERY ADMINISTRATION THAT COUNTS ON HIM TO MAKE PEACE"**
*May 3, 1983*

Iran is one of the many fascinating places in the Middle East. Iranian women march to support their national leader, to uphold their right to be totally veiled and subordinated—and for the right to send their little children to be killed in battle. It would be nice to say goodbye to the quaint leaders of Iran—and while we're in the neighborhood, we could also say goodbye to the leaders of Iraq, Syria and Libya, friends of terrorists. Governments of some countries vaguely described as Third World have sent plenty of people into the next world.

Several Middle East governments bade farewell to Yasser Arafat, leader of the Palestine Liberation Organization (PLO), one of several armed groups in Lebanon. His army had occupied much of Beirut before the Israeli army moved into Lebanon in 1982. Most of his Arab neighbors pulled in the welcome mat when he was looking for a new headquarters. But he was eventually welcomed back, warmly embraced by Arab leaders and set up shop in Tunisia.

After investigations of the massacres at two Palestinian camps that were supposedly under Israeli protection, the Israeli government said goodbye to Ariel Sharon as Defense Minister—but hello to him in a new cabinet position. A sad and weary Prime Minister Menachem Begin later said goodbye to his duties as Prime Minister.

For many years, King Hussein of Jordan has been on the verge of wanting to do something for peace in the Middle East—on alternate Tuesdays. He is regarded as a great friend of the United States because he speaks English, he married an American woman, and at one time reportedly accepted CIA funds.

Some day, when the wind is from the right direction and when he has the complete support of all Arab countries, he might join a peace effort.

Iran, Iraq and Saudi Arabia are among the members of the Organization of Petroleum Exporting Countries (OPEC). This organization, which has never boasted many democracies in its membership, created the oil shocks of the 1970s that increased inflation and very nearly destabilized the industrial democracies of the world. Perhaps more significantly, it destabilized Third World oil importers, leading to severe debt crises. With a decline in oil prices, the rulers of most

**"THEY TEND TO SPOIL THE EFFECT A LITTLE"**

*July 20, 1982*

**"IT'LL BLOW OVER—IT'LL BLOW OVER—"**

*October 6, 1982*

**"THAT SOLVES THE PROBLEM OF HOW TO DEAL WITH AUTHORITARIAN REGIMES"**

*July 2, 1981*

**"ONE LITTLE MURDER AND EVERYBODY GETS ALL UPSET"**

*October 4, 1983*

of these countries have had to be satisfied with oil profits that are merely exorbitant instead of outrageous.

Government officials and businessmen frequently visit these quaint countries. Some of our most active world travelers in recent years have been American vice presidents, who fill in at funerals and other occasions that are not on the president's schedule. During Nelson Rockefeller's term as vice president someone asked him what future trips he would be taking, and he said, "Well, that depends on who dies."

Vice President Bush, our official mission-to-Moscow-funerals man, also made some less somber trips. He might better have skipped his visit to the Philippines in 1981 or at least visited it in golden silence. Bush told President Ferdinand Marcos that "We love your adherence to democratic principles and to democratic processes."

Over the years, Marcos had skillfully guided his country from democracy to dictatorship. And when democratic leader Benigno Aquino decided to return to the Philippines to promote freedom, Imelda Marcos warned Aquino that he would probably be killed. She was right. Aquino was gunned down just as he was debarking from his plane, before he had a chance to set foot again on his native soil. The airport was completely under the Marcos government's control, and Aquino was completely surrounded by Marcos' soldiers at the time. The Marcoses have been so prophetic about hazards to life and about election returns that it is eerie. We can easily bid them farewell, something a majority of Philippine people would probably like to do also.

Now to the cooler climate of the Soviet Union and its satellite countries. There was not only a chill in relations between us and them, but a chill within the eastern bloc itself—where the Russians have had to use a cold and heavy hand to keep everyone in line. When the rulers of the U.S.S.R. didn't confess to a mistake in the downing of Korean Air Lines passenger plane 007, their minds seemed to be icing up. And when they drew an additional iron curtain around Nobel physicist Andrei Sakharov and his wife Yelena Bonner, it was difficult to avoid the impression that in the cold war the Kremlin leaders' heads had frozen solid.

*May 22, 1984*

**ALBATROSS**
*September 25, 1983*

**"INTERNAL MATTER"**
*December 17, 1981*

**"ANOTHER NOBEL PRIZE!"**
*October 6, 1983*

The U.S.S.R. has not relaxed its grip on Poland or on dissenters. But on the other hand it has not been able to choke off their desire for freedom.

The Kremlin rulers and the Reagan administration seemed determined not to be outdumb by each other. There is no comparison between our form of government and theirs. But under the recent leadership of both countries it is at least *possible* to see why some Europeans have felt "a plague o' both your houses!"

With the sun setting on the gilded domes of Moscow, we would like to say farewell to the Kremlin, Palace of Paranoia. But, despite Reagan's paraphrase of Bolshevik words, Marxism-Leninism in the Soviet Union is not likely to end up on the ash heap of history very soon. So far, we have only this one world to live in together, and we don't want to say goodbye to it.

Before our travelogue sinks into despair, let us have a look at sunny Spain, where democracy returned after the dark years under Hitler's ally, Generalissimo Francisco Franco. Under King Juan Carlos, Spain even survived an attempted coup by generals longing for the bad old days. Olé!

A way back in history it was Spanish ships that first arrived to discover Latin America. But the United States can claim to have discovered Latin America *more often* than anyone else has. We do it every four or eight years.

Every U.S. administration sooner or later discovers the rest of the hemisphere or discovers a new plan for it.

When Herbert Hoover was president-elect, he cruised around Latin America on a U.S. Navy ship.

Franklin Roosevelt inaugurated the "good neighbor" policy.

When Richard Nixon was vice president, he ran into trouble in Caracas, Venezuela.

John Kennedy established the Alliance for Progress.

But President Reagan made the most amazing discovery. In December 1982, he returned from a five-day trip to Latin America, with which he had previously been unfamiliar. He said that his trip had been "real fruitful" and that he "learned a lot." And finally he said: "You'd be surprised. They're all individual countries."

**"OUR NEIGHBORS MUST HELP KEEP
THE BRITISH FROM DISTURBING OUR
PEACE"**

*April 21, 1982*

**"SEE THEM BLINK YET?"**

*April 27, 1982*

**"RIGHT, CHIEF—WE STICK TO A
MIDDLE COURSE BETWEEN SOUND
JUDGMENT AND COMPLETE IDIOCY"**

*April 7, 1982*

**"MY FOLKS DON'T UNDERSTAND ME"**

*June 2, 1982*

This recent discovery of individual countries south of Mexico is probably one of the most remarkable ever. And it may live on when questions are raised about the foreign policy qualifications of future presidential and vice presidential candidates.

Some of those individual countries might wish Reagan had left them undiscovered.

Latin America came sharply to the world's attention in April 1982, when the military dictatorship of Argentina, under President Leopoldo Galtieri, seized the British Falkland Islands.

President Reagan was unable to reach Galtieri on the phone because the general delayed receiving the call until his troops were well on their way.

The Reagan administration had been friendly to Galtieri. On April 2, 1982, the evening *after* the Falklands invasion was launched, our United Nations ambassador, Jeane Kirkpatrick, was the guest of honor at a dinner at the Argentine embassy.

The U.S. followed a policy that was even-handed though not level-headed. It pursued a firm muddle course, with Reagan saying about the British government and the Argentine dictatorship that "We're friends with both." While Prime Minister Margaret Thatcher dispatched a British fleet to retake the Falklands, Secretary of State Alexander Haig hoped to serve as mediator.

Belatedly, the U.S. government sided with the British government —a decision that could have made a difference had it been articulated at the very beginning.

Later, when Thatcher did not support the U.S. invasion of Grenada, United States Information Agency director Charles Z. Wick put his mind to work on the subject. He said the reason she didn't support our invasion was because she was a woman.

Argentina was the country of "the disappeared"—the nation where people were taken away by the government to be shot through the head or sometimes dropped from planes. The number of these "disappeareds" may have been between 8,000 and 20,000. But the defeat in the Falklands was too much even for the military. They deposed Galtieri and called for an election—which was won by Raul Alfonsin. The new government arrested Galtieri and other generals.

President Reagan made another of his discoveries in Central

**"TELL YOUR PRESIDENT TO SEND
SOME CORONERS TOO, DOCTOR"**
*June 14, 1983*

**"WHAT'S THE GOOD OF BEING
COMMANDER-IN-CHIEF IF YOU CAN'T
EVEN HAVE SECRET WARS?"**
*May 5, 1983*

**"EH?"**
*April 6, 1983*

**UNDERCOVER OPERATION**
*January 6, 1983*

America—that trouble in the region was all due to Russian and Cuban interference, and that U.S. military solutions were the answer.

In El Salvador, the killings of civilians by "death squads" and military groups exceeded the number of government troops killed by leftist revolutionaries. In 1984, the far-rightist Robert d'Aubuisson, generally considered to be connected with the killings of civilians, was defeated in an election for President of El Salvador by moderate José Napoleon Duarte. But under the sponsorship of Sen. Jesse Helms (R-N.C.) d'Aubuisson came to Washington and made speeches. The Reagan administration, which had previously denied a visa to d'Aubuisson, now gave him one. In its visa policies, the administration had most often sheltered people of the U.S. from hearing the views of Latin Americans it considered too far to the left, including a number of writers.

On Nicaragua, Congress at first reluctantly approved the Reagan administration's support of the "contras"—a mixed group of anti-Sandinistas. Some had helped to overthrow the dictatorship of Anastasio Somoza and had become disillusioned. Some were "Somozists" who had fought the revolution from the start.

The Reagan administration maintained that it was not trying to overthrow the Marxist Sandinista government of Nicaragua. But it just happened to aid people who were trying to overthrow the Marxist Sandinista government of Nicaragua.

Its explanations for what it was doing included pressuring the Sandinistas to change their foreign and domestic policies, and trying to stop the steady flow of arms to El Salvador's leftist rebels.

But the steady flow of arms to El Salvador rebels was not proven convincingly, and over 40 percent of the rebel arms consisted of U.S. weapons captured or bought from the El Salvador government forces.

The U.S. policy in Central America got to be too much for Congress when it learned that our overt-covert war against Nicaragua included the mining of that country's harbors. This mining, done under the generalship of CIA director William J. Casey, resulted in damage to some foreign ships. His not-so-secret military operations were not-so-successful.

**"HOW IS IT THAT THEIR GUERRILLAS SEEM TO DO SO MUCH BETTER THAN OUR GUERRILLAS?"**

*July 29, 1983*

**"THERE HE GOES AGAIN"**

*April 13, 1984*

**"KIDS! SEE IF YOU CAN GUESS WHERE ELSE THE BUNNY HAS BEEN LAYING EGGS"**

*April 17, 1984*

**"LOOK OUT FOR SUBVERSIVES"**

*May 23, 1984*

The mining of Nicaraguan harbors was called off. And in mid-1984 the House of Representatives, for the second year in a row, voted against further aid to the contras.

Had Reagan been less partisan or one who could acknowledge a mistake, he might have thanked President Jimmy Carter for having negotiated and won Senate approval of the Panama Canal treaties.

These agreements, like the nuclear and arms control treaties, had been opposed by candidate Ronald Reagan. His troubles in Central America and the dangers to American interests there were probably small compared to the possibilities of what would have happened if relations with Panama had deteriorated.

As it was, Panama—along with Venezuela, Mexico and Colombia —formed a group that tried to negotiate a settlement in Central America. Reagan's lip service to their peace efforts was not as loud as his planes and tanks.

The administration expressed concern about protecting democracy in Latin America. But it failed to come to grips with a problem here at home that was of vital interest to debtor nations there. The skyrocketing U.S. federal deficit pushed up interest rates that hurt our friends to the south.

In the 1920s, when our former allies were being squeezed by war debts owed to the U.S., Calvin Coolidge said cooly, "They hired the money, didn't they?"

As an admirer of Coolidge and of gunboat diplomacy, Reagan might have felt the same way. Certainly he could have shown more imagination in dealing with our Latin friends—especially with a new Argentine democracy that was struggling to make its way out of inherited financial crises.

But solutions to their money problems would not have involved arms. It might even have required cuts in our arms programs to bring deficits and interest rates into line. Unthinkable!

Well, if democracy should sink slowly in the south, we could bid it a fond farewell. But what an opportunity to send more weapons, more advisers, and even more troops to Latin America to revive democracy there!

We could be off to new adventures again.  ■

**SUCCESSOR TO THE POWDER KEG**
*September 24, 1980*

**ARABIAN NIGHTMARE**
*July 16, 1982*

**"—OR I MIGHT WEAR THIS ONE—"**
*April 20, 1983*

**LIFE BY THE SWORD**
*September 1, 1981*

**"WELCOME ABOARD—I'M GLAD TO
TAKE ALL OF YOU FOR A RIDE"**
*October 10, 1980*

**"EVERYBODY OUT OF LEBANON BUT
THE LEBANESE? WHAT ARE YOU,
SOME KIND OF NUT?"**
*June 11, 1982*

**"YOU WANT TO SEE US, FRIEND?"**
*June 15, 1980*

**"UNFORTUNATELY—"**
*April 12, 1983*

**"YOU CAN SEE HE'S VERY FOND OF CHILDREN"**

*August 6, 1982*

**WEAPON OF DEMOCRACY**

*February 9, 1983*

**AERIAL GAME**

*August 25, 1981*

**"KINDA GETS YOU ALL CHOKED UP, DOESN'T IT?"**

*March 8, 1983*

**"DAMNED PROLETARIAT"**
*August 31, 1980*

*June 21, 1983*

*December 31, 1981*

**"I TOLD YOU IT WOULD JUST BE A
SUSPENSION"**
*October 17, 1982*

**"SOLIDARITY IS PLOTTING TO TURN THIS INTO SOME KIND OF DAY FOR THE WORKING CLASS"**
*April 21, 1983*

**AN AWARD FOR GEN. JARUZELSKI**
*December 15, 1983*

**"SURELY YOU WON'T MIND WEARING THIS PRESS CARD AROUND YOUR NECK"**
*May 20, 1981*

**"OLÉ"**
*February 25, 1981*

**"BUT YOU CAN STILL TAKE PART IN THE CONTINUING SPECIAL EVENTS IN AFGHANISTAN"**

*May 9, 1984*

**"THE AFGHANS SENT IT TO CELEBRATE OUR THIRD ANNIVERSARY HERE"**

*December 28, 1982*

**SHOWING THE FLAG IN EL SALVADOR**

*March 1, 1981*

**"NO, SEÑOR, THEY ARE NOT DIGGING IN AGAINST GUERRILLAS—THEY ARE BURYING THEIR PEOPLE KILLED BY SALVADORAN DEATH SQUADS"**

*October 12, 1983*

**"THEY'RE RUNNING SO SHORT OF BULLETS, THEY'VE EVEN HAD TO CUT DOWN ON SHOOTING THEIR CIVILIANS"**

*March 9, 1983*

**"AND NOW—"**

*July 19, 1983*

**"I HATE TELLING T.R. THINGS LIKE THIS—HE WANTS TO GO BACK TO THE WHITE HOUSE AND RAISE HELL"**

*April 8, 1984*

**"WELL, NOBODY CAN ACCUSE US OF BEING ONE-SIDED"**

*March 29, 1984*

**"ANOTHER ONE SUSPECTED OF
EATING QUICHE"**
*June 1, 1983*

**"BOOM!"**
*April 12, 1984*

**"WE HAVE TO BE READY TO COPE
WITH THOSE ANTI-DEMOCRATIC
FORCES OVER THERE"**
*March 18, 1984*

**THE OPEN MOUTHS**
*May 30, 1984*

"WE ARE INDEPENDENT OF THE WHITE HOUSE"

*January 18, 1984*

# AND JUSTICE FOR ALL

H istorians must be something like archaeologists, sifting through
layer beneath layer, fitting pieces together—and always knowing that
pieces are missing. It is hard enough to keep up with events from day
to day, or to recapture those of a year or two ago. Politicians count
on this. The mouth is quicker than the eye—or the memory. Such
thoughts occur on reading through speeches of not too long ago.

On Nov. 2, 1983, in the White House Rose Garden, President
Reagan signed into law the bill establishing an annual holiday honor-
ing Martin Luther King, Jr.

The remarks Reagan read on that occasion were beautiful and
moving. He said: "In America, in the fifties and sixties, one of the
important crises we faced was racial discrimination. The man whose
words and deeds in that crisis stirred our nation to its very soul was
Dr. Martin Luther King, Jr." He told about rules that had required
blacks to sit in the backs of buses and how Rosa Parks, told to move
to the back, had said, "No." And he recalled King's never-to-be-
forgotten words, "I have a dream . . ."

Among presidential papers the words will read well.

"SINCE THAT SIGN'S BEEN UP,
THERE'S BEEN SO FEW ACCIDENTS
WE DON'T NEED IT ANY MORE"
*June 30, 1981*

"YOU PEOPLE DON'T APPRECIATE
HOW FIRMLY THE APPOINTEES OF
THIS ADMINISTRATION HAVE
ALWAYS OPPOSED LYNCHING"
*June 2, 1983*

"IT MIGHT BE THAT WE COULD HAVE
HANDLED THIS SITUATION BETTER"
*January 21, 1982*

"FREE AT LAST. FREE AT LAST—"
*October 20, 1983*

But future historians may have a hard time matching those words with other words and deeds. Looking back a few pages in the presidential papers they would find an Oct. 19 news conference Q and A:

> Q. Mr. President, Senator Helms has been saying on the Senate floor that Martin Luther King, Jr., had Communist associations, was a Communist sympathizer. Do you agree?
> A. We'll know in about 35 years, won't we? . . .

The "we'll know in about 35 years" referred to the time lapse before the opening of FBI papers compiled under the stewardship of J. Edgar Hoover, who saw communists everywhere, who hated and feared blacks—King most of all. Hoover called Martin Luther King "the most notorious liar in the country" and even hoped to get King to commit suicide. It would not take 35 years or 35 minutes to know the value of this material collected by Hoover after he had been too long in office. It did not take 35 seconds to know that the presidential remark was offensive.

A reader of Reagan's eloquent remarks on signing the King holiday bill would not know either that this president had opposed Congress' strengthening of the Voting Rights Act before he signed it in 1983.

Writing about the administration's preference for a bill without the new wording, Steven V. Roberts reported in *The New York Times* on April 28, 1983:

> The Administration has been lobbying heavily for a version of the bill, basically an extension of the existing law, that liberals say would make it harder for members of minorities to prove that they had been victims of discrimination. According to several Senate sources, Administration officials, led by Attorney General William French Smith, have been arguing that a basic extension of the law would serve the interests of the Republican Party because members of minorities generally vote for Democrats.

Reagan's Rose Garden speech also referred to the great progress represented by the civil rights acts of 1964 and 1965. The reader in 1983 would not have guessed that he opposed those measures at the time—saying that he was in favor of their goals but that they were bad legislation. And it might have come as a surprise that he had also

**BACK OF THE BUS**
*December 5, 1980*

**"OF COURSE, YOU REALIZE WE ONLY
TOOK THIS ACTION SO THAT
CONGRESS COULD VOTE AGAINST IT"**
*January 13, 1982*

**"GOLLY, I'VE BEEN SO BUSY
DEMANDING COMPLETE
INVESTIGATIONS AND FIGHTING
DISCRIMINATION AND BEING FAIR
TO WOMEN AND POOR PEOPLE AND
SCHOOL CHILDREN . . . "**
*July 13, 1983*

**"TELL YOU WHAT—WE MIGHT
APPROVE BUSING IF YOU'LL SIT IN
THE BACK"**
*August 11, 1982*

opposed fair housing legislation before its passage in 1968. However, as a candidate in 1980 he said that "it is institutionalized and it has, let's say, hastened the solutions of a lot of problems."

We can more easily recall recent events. Since the early 1970s, the federal government had withheld funds from private schools that practiced racial discrimination—a policy upheld by federal courts. But in January 1982, the Reagan administration decided that such schools should be given tax exemptions. The most famous of these was Bob Jones University of Greenville, S.C.

The Justice Department, under William French Smith, went to court to argue for the administration's policy. The Supreme Court ruled against the administration, upholding the pre-Reagan government policy.

The Reagan administration strenuously opposed busing for school desegregation. From the intensity of its opposition, you would have thought school buses were some diabolical new invention by which children would be whisked away never to be seen again.

The administration also dragged its feet on affirmative action programs. In each case, the Justice Department discussed legalities to support its positions; and in each case, members of minority groups found the U.S. Department of Justice was not on their side.

The late Clarence Mitchell, prominent civil rights leader, wrote in 1984:

> When the Congress passed the 1964 Civil Rights Act it included Title IX, which authorized the attorney general to make the government a party to private suits seeking to vindicate civil rights where the claim of discrimination is based on race.
>
> At the time Title IX was added it is unlikely that anyone could have anticipated that the Justice Department would seriously argue that voluntary actions taken by state and local governments to end longstanding patterns of racial discrimination should be voided because of discrimination against whites.
>
> This latest action by the Reagan team makes one wonder whether the administration is suffering from amnesia about the years of struggle that culminated in civil rights laws passed during this century.

While the administration might argue that such things as jobs are not necessarily "rights," minorities could not help but notice that the unemployment statistics were also against them.

**"IT'S A FREE COUNTRY UNTIL YOU DECIDE TO GO OUT OF IT"**
*July 5, 1981*

**"RIGHT BEHIND YOU"**
*March 26, 1982*

**"LUCKY WE'RE DOING THIS—WE'VE ALREADY CAUGHT SOME WHO REALLY BELIEVE IN CIVIL RIGHTS"**
*April 26, 1983*

**"GIMME THAT—WE DON'T WANT YOU POOR FOLKS THROWING YOUR WEIGHT AROUND"**
*June 19, 1981*

One of Reagan's longtime targets was the federal Legal Services Corporation (LSC), an agency providing legal assistance to the poor. The administration made every effort to destroy this service. It tried to cut off all funds, but Congress provided enough to keep the agency going. Reagan then appointed LSC board members during Senate recesses to avoid their having to face the required approval by the Senate.

Another administration target was the Civil Rights Commission, which had no enforcement power but spoke with moral authority. President Nixon replaced Father Theodore Hesburgh of Notre Dame with Dr. Arthur Fleming as head of the commission in 1972. But whatever Nixon's intent, the commission continued as the voice of conscience.

President Reagan went much further. He tried to destroy the commission and failed. Attempts to stack it ran into congressional opposition. Then it seemed that a compromise had finally been reached, which would leave previous appointees in a majority. But with help from Republican senators, Reagan managed to get a controlling number of members. The commission continued to exist but no longer as the independent agency it was created to be.

Advocates of civil liberties and civil rights who were disturbed about this could also be concerned about something else.

After such concentrated effort to still dissent in a commission without power, what would Reagan do if several Supreme Court appointments fell his way? On the present Court, the scales were already tilting in favor of The Authorities as opposed to the rights of the individual.

There were earlier warnings about administration policies on rights and liberties. In 1981, presidential adviser Edwin Meese had spoken of the American Civil Liberties Union as a "criminals' lobby." And Attorney General Smith, speaking in October of that year, gave his views on the courts.

He said, "We believe that the groundswell of conservatism evidenced by the 1980 election makes this an especially appropriate time to urge upon the courts" that they "diminish judicial activism." He said that the Court had "weighted the balance in favor of individual interests against the decisions of state and Federal legislatures." And

**"YOU SEE, WE'RE AGAINST BUSES
BECAUSE THEY MIGHT ENCOURAGE
'WHITE FLIGHT' "**

*August 25, 1982*

**"WE TOLD YOU WE BELIEVED IN
PRIVATE INITIATIVE, DIDN'T WE?"**

*April 16, 1982*

**"JUST BETWEEN US IN THE FAMILY—"**

*April 25, 1982*

**"I'D LIKE TO TELL A FEW THINGS TO
THAT JUDGE'S PARENTS"**

*February 17, 1983*

he wanted to "return the courts to a more principled deference to the actions of the elected branches."

When Finley Peter Dunne had Mr. Dooley say that "th' supreme coort follows th' iliction returns," he could hardly have foreseen that a future attorney general would feel that Dooley's humorous comment of an earlier day should describe the function of the Supreme Court.

Smith was demanding "judicial restraint" from courts whose duty it was to see that other branches of government exercised proper restraint in matters affecting basic rights and liberties.

As for activism, the administration had no complaints on 1984 decisions in its favor, even when the Supreme Court reached far beyond immediate cases to set long-range policy. Judicial "activism" is in the eye of the beholder.

Another Smith objective was to "redress the imbalance between the forces of law and the forces of lawlessness."

But there seemed to be different scales for the poor and for the well-to-do, especially those who were "right" politically. In such cases justice could be tempered with mercy.

It was Ronald Reagan who had said of the Watergate conspirators that they were "not criminals at heart."

In July 1983, Reagan delivered a speech on freedom and justice. But he made it before the politically friendly International Longshoremen's Association (ILA), which had been notorious for terrorism on the waterfront.

In the previous six years, 20 ILA officials, including ten vice presidents, were convicted of charges including racketeering and extortion.

But the ILA had supported Reagan for President in 1980 and continued its support of him.

In the same month that he addressed the ILA, Reagan created a commission on organized crime and said, "It's time to break the power of the mob in America."

Reagan not only maintained his ties to the ILA, but also enjoyed the support of the Teamsters union, which had long been one of the largest and most corrupt in the country. It was for corruption that the AFL-CIO had expelled it. Three of the Teamsters' last four presidents were convicted of crimes.

**"HEY, RON—IT'S ME!"**
*December 2, 1981*

**"DO YOU THINK THEY SHOULD HAVE FOUND THAT WOMAN GUILTY OF BEING RAPED?"**
*March 23, 1984*

**"BEFORE YOU FOLD THAT TENT AND SILENTLY STEAL AWAY—"**
*March 12, 1982*

*May 2, 1984*

**"SOB SISTER"**

*March 4, 1982*

*August 29, 1982*

**"IT'S ALL RIGHT BECAUSE THEY'RE SINCERE"**

*December 6, 1978*

**"AND, LORD, CURSE THOSE HEATHEN JUSTICES WHO DO NOT SHARE THE FINE CHRISTIAN VALUES OF OUR PRESIDENT"**

*May 25, 1983*

For all their talk about law and justice, Reagan and his attorney general had remarkable tolerance for the misdeeds of supporters—including those within the administration.

Even in the area of street violence, an administration concerned with curbing crime might have wanted to do something about the proliferation of small handguns. But the Reagan administration also numbered among its political constituents the National Rifle Association (NRA), and went right down the line with NRA policies.

When he was running for president, Reagan had condemned a government that "has become more intrusive, more coercive, more meddlesome and less effective."

But as president, he approved domestic surveillance and black-bag jobs by government agents.

In the 1984 case of Baby Jane Doe, a Long Island couple was harried because of Reagan administration efforts to make the hospital that treated their handicapped child produce its medical records. The parents felt they and the doctors and the hospital had made the best decision they could. And the courts repeatedly rejected intrusive demands for the records. In this Big Brother activity, the Department of Justice claimed it wanted to make sure the infant was not being discriminated against.

The same Reagan who was opposed to "more intrusive" and "more meddlesome" government never tired of meddling with America's local public schools and intruding his ideas for organized prayer.

His administration tried to enforce a "squeal rule" for girls seeking prescription birth-control devices, and it advocated an end to legal abortions. An administration concerned about terror seemed to have a hard time finding tongue to condemn the bombing and other violence at abortion clinics. And while speaking against "big government," it consistently threw its weight on the side of big government against the small individual. Wherever the Supreme Court whittled down protections for the individual, the administration was on the side of such "judicial restraint."

But the presidential speeches about patriotism and splendid deeds went on unrestrained. Years from now some of them will make fine reading.

They might even be read by schoolchildren, after they recite the Pledge of Allegiance to "one nation . . . indivisible . . ."  ∎

# THE PEOPLE'S CHOICE!

Sometimes it seems that the time spent on presidential campaigning is an eternity; but that's just an impression. Actually it's longer than that.

The race for the 1984 Democratic nomination, for example, began with the formation of the earth, went through the ice age and the building of the pyramids, the landing at Plymouth Rock, and the invention of television—and then began picking up steam for the long haul.

The entire election campaign had to end by January 20, 1985—if there was no dispute about the outcome—and by that time the 1988 race would be well on its way.

The candidates who are not incumbent presidents end up exhausted. So does the public, which has been running right along with them all the way, hoping to find a TV channel that is not doing advance speculation or post-mortems on caucuses or primaries—with full panels of predictors and endless polls.

The polls are all subject to change without notice, and generally do.

*March 25, 1976*

**"I DISAGREE WITH YOUR OPENING
STATEMENT—MY CANDIDATE WAS
WORSE THAN YOURS"**
*October 29, 1980*

**MEANWHILE, BACK AT THE RANCH—**
*October 31, 1980*

**"WE'RE ALL HERE, GRANDPA"**
*November 13, 1980*

The scriptural "to everything there is a season" was written before there were two nationwide football leagues and before modern presidential campaigning. We get enough interviews, polls and analysis for everybody to O.D. long before election day.

But if people get tired of presidential campaigns, their interest in presidents never flags. Presidents DO go on forever—in the history books, in their own presidential libraries, and in the royal treatment now given ex-presidents.

After they leave office, they and their families get aides, bodyguards, pensions, and money allowances that might have made the founders wonder what kind of royalty or ex-royalty they had helped to establish.

No matter how able an almost-president, close doesn't count. A president, however inept, undistinguished or even crooked, is always —TA ta de-TAH tah—A President. And we want to know all about him.

Of course, that doesn't mean they all have to be re-elected, although this is an idea that has gained some headway, too.

Some political observers bemoan the lack of recent two-term presidents, suggesting that the public is fickle or that people are out to "break" presidents—as if every president were *entitled* to two terms.

But it was not a fickle public that deprived John F. Kennedy of a second term. It was an assassin.

It was Lyndon Johnson's own decision, during the long, divisive Vietnam War, not to seek a second full term—after having served almost a term and a half.

It was Richard Nixon's culpability in crimes that caused him to resign before finishing a second term.

Gerald Ford was not an elected president although he nearly became one.

The term is for four years, and then it's up to the voters again.

Furthermore, the president has a built-in advantage in running for re-election. Renomination is generally his for the asking. And with all the ceremonies, the camera shots, the non-political trips that include political speeches, and the ability to make news, the prospects for re-election are always good unless he blows it.

**"GOODNESS KNOWS, WE WENT THE EXTRA MILE"**

*April 30, 1982*

**"WE'RE PRETTY WELL BOOKED FOR 1984—WOULD YOU CARE TO LEAVE YOUR NAME FOR 1988?"**

*February 27, 1983*

**"AND THEN THERE'S THOSE DARN PEOPLE LIKE THE ONES IN SOUTH SUCCOTASH WHO VOTED FOR ME"**

*March 21, 1982*

**"AND WE THOUGHT SOME PRODUCT COMMERCIALS WERE OFFENSIVE"**

*April 21, 1981*

Jimmy Carter's downfall probably began when he made himself the prisoner of the hostage situation in Iran—vowing not to leave the White House to campaign until the hostages were freed. This self-confinement may have been conceived as a clever political strategy. But the number of days before the hostages were released turned out to be the same number of days before Carter left the White House.

Debates have become pretty standard fare for presidential candidates, generally with a few memorable lines or fluffs.

President Ford's classification of Poland as a country not under the domination of the U.S.S.R. probably helped Carter win the election.

Reagan, after hurting himself by sitting out a 1980 debate among Republican candidates, came back with a good line at Nashua, New Hampshire, when his words paraphrased those in the movie "State of the Union." He said, "I *paid* for this microphone, Mr. Green."

President Carter's references to his little daughter Amy's thoughts on nuclear proliferation scored no points in his debate with Reagan.

And Reagan's "There you go again" went well, even if we don't remember what it referred to.

In his closing statement, Reagan used an old favorite—lines from a 1630 sermon by Gov. John Winthrop: ". . . we shall be a city on a hill . . ." Reagan had burnished it by making it "a *shining* city on a hill." It sounded beautiful—even if he later gave us a shoddy government in Washington.

Presidential campaigns give us special words. In 1980, the big word was *momentum*. In the 1984 primaries, the word was *volatile*. In every campaign, a big word is *expectations*—how a candidate is expected to score in a caucus or primary. Sen. Edmund Muskie, a vice presidential candidate in 1968 and later a presidential aspirant, touched on something politically vital when he spoke of *perceptions* —how voters *perceive* things.

In the 1972 New Hampshire primary a campaign aide had unwisely predicted such a big win for Muskie that the candidate was *perceived* to be losing because his victory did not come up to *expectations*.

Some drugs are said to heighten perceptions, and television does the same.

**"ACTUALLY, I THINK IT CAME BEFORE THE VIDEO GAME"**
*May 20, 1982*

**"ONE OF YOUR GREATEST ACTING JOBS, CHIEF"**
*October 5, 1982*

**"I DIDN'T COME TO WASHINGTON TO PLAY POLITICS-AS-USUAL"**
*October 26, 1982*

**"READY TO VOTE FOR A CHANGE IN THIS LEADERSHIP?"**
*November 9, 1980*

Ford began the SALT II talks but was probably remembered more for trying to fight inflation with a WIN button.

Despite successes such as the Camp David agreements, the Panama Canal treaties and the normalization of relations with China, President Carter was not perceived as a leader, particularly as his term wore on.

President Reagan, with acting and speaking ability, strode around looking and sounding like a true leader, even when he was waffling, shifting ground, or figuratively falling on his face.

In the 1984 primary campaign, former Vice President Walter Mondale found himself tagged as a candidate of "special interests" by his opponents as well as by President Reagan—though Reagan represented the big money interests and Mondale's Democratic rivals had sought the endorsements he got.

The nominating process and the campaign of 1984, which seemed longer than recorded history, are worth a few words, and I'll start with some strong ones. I think it's plain awful that the Iowa caucuses and the New Hampshire primary play a political role of such exaggerated importance. There have been efforts to bring states into line to avoid this Hey-lookee-First-in-the-nation selection. But every four years, candidates and news people practically outnumber the voters in those two states.

The best solution I know of was offered by political writer Michael Barone. He suggests that about six other states or state parties should not set a definite date for their primaries but simply say they will hold them on the same day as New Hampshire's.

Even the balloting in a group of primaries a couple of weeks later doesn't undo the influence of those early contests.

In 1984, the voters of California were delighted to find that they still had something to say about who was nominated—though not a great deal. Several candidates had been eliminated long before.

In 1983, organizations such as the AFL-CIO and the National Education Association broke precedent to endorse a presidential candidate before the primaries. They hoped to unite the party behind an acceptable candidate and eliminate a long, wearing struggle for the Democratic nomination. Their candidate, Mondale, eventually

*October 15, 1982*

**THE LAST PICTURE SHOW**
*October 27, 1982*

**"HANG IN THERE"**
*October 19, 1982*

**"WHAT'S IT DONE TO THE CONTENTS OF *THIS* BOX?"**
*November 2, 1982*

was successful in the primaries and caucuses, but things didn't work out as anticipated.

After winning in Iowa, Mondale slipped up in New Hampshire, where the voters may have thought he took them for granite. It could have been that Mondale in his tailored topcoat looked too much like a buttoned-up candidate who thought he had the nomination buttoned up too. Sen. Gary Hart pulled a stunning upset, and the long battle was on.

Mondale might have forgotten an old political rule that I just made up: Nobody gets to be president by acting more presidential than the president. Every successful candidate from Roosevelt to Reagan has known the advantage of appearing easy, spontaneous and informal. When Hart was photographed wearing a lumberjack shirt and suspenders and tossing an ax, it may have had nothing to do with the campaign for the presidency—or with Hart himself—but it looked refreshing.

In the next two batches of primaries, five of the eight candidates dropped out, and then there were three: Mondale, Hart and Jesse Jackson, who drew many votes that might have given Mondale an early win.

Jackson was the unquestioned phenomenon of 1984. He had no hope of winning the nomination, but staying in the race enabled him to share the spotlight with the two leading candidates. He was *news*, and he made the most of it.

Jackson's candidacy was, in a way, the flip side of George Wallace's a few campaigns earlier. Although Jackson had never held public office, he proved to be a skillful operator and a lively campaigner—with a strong racial appeal.

His early theme was "Our time has come!" And he told followers in Chicago, "We picked their cotton! We cooked their food! We ironed their clothing! We nursed their babies! Now we can run their cities! We can run their states! We will run their nation!"

The Jackson campaign hit a snag when it was disclosed, in *The Washington Post,* on Feb. 13, 1984, that in conversations with Milton Coleman and other black reporters he referred to Jews as "Hymies" and to New York as "Hymietown."

*November 4, 1982*

"ASK THE WHITE HOUSE IF WE CAN
CATCH ANYTHING FROM SHAKING
HANDS WITH HER"

*January 5, 1983*

"THAT'S FUNNY—I WAS SURE IT SAID
SOMETHING ABOUT A REVOLUTION"

*November 7, 1982*

"FORWARD! FORWARD! FORWARD!
WAIT FOR YOUR LEADER, MEN!"

*November 26, 1982*

In response to questions about those remarks, he said, "I'm not familiar with that. That's not accurate." But when the questions didn't go away, he finally acknowledged almost two weeks later that he had been quoted accurately. However, he then said that he hadn't lied in his previous disclaimers.

One of Jackson's explanations for his "Hymie" references was that when he was a kid, people used to talk about going to "Jewtown" and bargaining with "Hymie." If a non-black candidate had talked about "coons" and used the excuse that when he was a kid, he heard people talk about "coontown," he would have been told quickly that he was not a kid any more—or a presidential candidate either.

Over the years there had been Jackson slurs about Jewish reporters and Jewish labor leaders. In 1973 he said about Nixon's top advisers that "four out of five of them are German Jews"—apparently under the impression that H. R. Haldeman and John Ehrlichman fit the description.

The "Hymie" episode took on a new dimension when Jackson's close ally and longtime supporter, Louis Farrakhan, weighed in. Farrakhan, leader of the "Nation of Islam" movement, said in a broadcast, "We are going to make an example of Coleman. One day soon we are going to punish you with death. We are going to punish the traitor and make the traitor beg for forgiveness." He went on to declare that the reporter's wife would also be punished if she continued to live with Coleman.

Instead of denouncing the threat, Jackson acted as if it had occurred in some distant land. He said of Farrakhan that "I respect him very much" and that what happened was a "conflict" between "two very able professionals caught in a cycle that could be damaging to their careers." And he suggested that the two men get together, with himself mediating their "dispute."

Coleman was indeed a "very able professional." He was threatened by one of Jackson's principal allies, who appeared on platforms with Jackson and who provided Jackson with Nation of Islam bodyguards.

The conflict was not between Farrakhan and Coleman—or between blacks and Jews—any more than Bull Connor's treatment of

**"CONSTANT DRUMBEAT"**
*July 28, 1983*

**"HOW CAN WE TELL IF HE'S RUNNING? WHEN HAS HE EVER MADE ANYTHING *BUT* POLITICAL SPEECHES?"**
*June 28, 1983*

**"BUT YOU'VE GOT TO ADMIT—IT'S UNDER HIS ADMINISTRATION THAT WE'RE BEGINNING TO PULL OUT OF THE REAGAN DEPRESSION"**
*May 22, 1983*

**"IT MIGHT BE THEIR SOLUTION TO THE UNEMPLOYMENT PROBLEM"**
*August 5, 1983*

blacks in Alabama was a difficulty between some blacks and some Southern whites. The conflict was between those who were willing to accept bigotry and those who opposed it.

In a later broadcast sermon, Farrakhan declared that Hitler was a great man—though wickedly great. And Jackson piously forgave his ally.

Politicians and interviewers generally treated Jackson gingerly. There were two reasons: (1) He was not taken seriously as a potential nominee; (2) He *was* taken seriously as a person with a large black following who would not hesitate to make his white critics appear anti-black—and black critics appear to be Uncle Toms.

But there was unquestionably genuine pride among many blacks in seeing a black candidate make a showing in a run to be nominated for President of the United States.

One of the ironies of the campaign was the talk of a "rainbow coalition." Mayors like Tom Bradley of Los Angeles and Wilson Goode of Philadelphia, elected in cities with large non-black populations, were the real mixers of colors, but it was Jackson, painting with a black palette, who *talked* rainbow.

Jackson also said that all "Hymie" wants to talk about is Israel. But it was Jackson who, when asked about statements that suggested bigotry in an American election, usually turned the subject to the Middle East.

Even before running for president Jackson had realized that all the world's a stage.

In September 1979, he went to the Middle East, where he made a point of embracing Yasser Arafat, leader of the Palestine Liberation Organization.

In 1983, on another trip to the Middle East, Jackson—accompanied by Farrakhan—met with Hafez Assad of Syria and secured the release of U.S. Navy flier Lt. Robert O. Goodman Jr.

In May 1984, Jackson started on a trip to Mexico, to Central America, and to see Fidel Castro in Cuba. He was there in mid-June when Farrakhan delivered a broadcast that was too much even for politicians who had been afraid to speak up. He called Judaism a "dirty religion," Israel an "outlaw state," and America, England,

**"GENDER GAP! THE WHOLE TROUBLE BEGAN WHEN THEY GOT THE VOTE"**

*August 9, 1983*

**"WE'RE SORRY BUT THIS IS HISPANIC MONTH"**

*October 16, 1983*

**"DO YOU THINK HE'LL STOP RUNNING?"**

*October 18, 1983*

**"STEP RIGHT UP—EVERYBODY GETS ONE STAR AND PART OF A STRIPE"**

*August 13, 1981*

and other nations that supported the creation of that state "criminals in the sight of Almighty God."

While he was in Havana, Jackson told CBS News, "In America people have freedom of speech. They can say what they want about what they want about whom they want. Don't keep putting me in the middle of that. Let me talk about peace in Central America."

His aides on the phone to Cuba apparently convinced Jackson that without a strong statement, his Latin American trip and his campaign were in serious trouble. So Jackson's aides read a statement that he had approved, saying that Farrakhan's words were "reprehensible and morally indefensible." On his return Jackson affirmed that it represented his view. By now Farrakhan was not a Jackson "surrogate" but a "supporter."

Jackson was always bold and often outrageous. He said that if he were white, he would be front-runner for the presidential nomination.

He refused to appear on a scheduled TV program with Julian Bond.

He refused to attend a dinner with George McGovern, Hart and Mondale, being held to promote unity and to help pay McGovern's campaign debts. He wrote an open letter belaboring McGovern.

McGovern's reply, which appeared on June 17, 1984, was a model of restraint. In it, he said:

> As a child I was told to "count to ten" before giving vent to anger. It has been more than 10 days since your June 3 open letter to me in the *Post* and your statements quoted in news stories accusing me of being "unprincipled and unfair" because I have not endorsed you for president. I haven't yet cooled off entirely but I'm ready to quit counting and start writing . . .

> I have never called another politician "unprincipled and unfair" simply because he didn't endorse me. If that were my tendency, I suppose I would have called you "unprincipled and unfair" for entering the nominating competition instead of endorsing me.

> But as you well know, I encouraged you to enter the race even after I was a candidate and welcomed your effort at every stage of your campaign. I criticized you only once, and that was

**"HOW LONG DO THEY GO ON?"**
*February 1, 1984*

**"AND NOW, FOLLOWING PHIL DONAHUE'S QUESTIONS, WE HAVE ANOTHER SHOW-BIZ SEGMENT FOR THE PRESIDENTIAL CANDIDATES"**
*January 17, 1984*

**"I'LL BE GLAD WHEN I CAN START RUNNING"**
*February 22, 1984*

*March 1, 1984*

not for anything you said about me but for your slur against Jews and your failure to promptly repudiate your spokesman after he described Hitler as a great man.

You say that it is not right for you to judge Louis Farrakhan. But you have not hesitated to judge me as "unprincipled" and as one who placed "pragmatism" above "conscience." But where are your principles and your conscience as a political leader and as a minister of the Gospel when you swallow a self-evident anti-Semitic bigot and life-threatening bully such as Louis Farrakhan? . . .

As the Democratic convention approached, Jackson suggested himself for secretary of state. He said that Jewish groups were responsible for the fact that Mondale did not consider him for the vice-presidential nomination. He asserted that "white women" had stolen his idea of a woman vice-presidential candidate and he attacked the "arrogant Aryan press."

Then, on a pre-convention TV program, he suddenly sounded contrite and conciliatory and he continued this tone when he addressed the Democratic convention.

But Jackson's divisiveness could be seen at that convention where his supporters booed Andrew Young—and later booed Coretta Scott King when she appeared before a black caucus. Young and King were both Mondale supporters.

Hart and Jackson partisans claimed that the Democratic Party rules cheated them out of convention delegates. But as columnist Mark Shields pointed out, 1984 supporters of both had been on the 1982 commission that set up the rules for this campaign. No minority reports were filed and no amendments were offered.

Since 1968 the Democrats have adopted successive rules changes in an effort to correct past deficiencies. And each time, somebody else was dissatisfied. Winner-take-all primaries were declared unfair by losers-who-got-nothing. A threshold of state primary votes to prevent party splintering was also criticized by those who didn't even get 20 percent of a divided vote.

As for primaries, at first there were too few and then there were too many. The fact is that losers are seldom happy, whatever the rules.

**"HOWEVER, I NOW HAVE AN
ANTI-SNAKE OIL"**

*February 3, 1984*

**"WE WEREN'T WATCHING—
ACTUALLY, WE'RE ALL PRIMARIED,
CAUCUSED, POLLED, PREDICTED,
DISCUSSED AND ANALYZED OUT"**

*March 22, 1984*

**"AND IF YOU DO THE SAME THINGS
THIS YEAR, I'LL COME THUNDERING
BACK AGAIN IN 1988"**

*March 30, 1984*

**NEW ENGLAND WINTER**

*March 6, 1984*

To get away from "bosses," rules were adopted that opened up the delegate selection and conventions. But—oops—these kept out many prominent office-holders, certainly entitled to seats. However, the 1984 rules seating office-holders brought the charges of robbing losing candidates of delegate seats. Long-shot candidates felt the rules worked against them.

The idea of a long shot being nominated for president, or vice president, is always appealing. But few would want to go back to smoke-filled rooms.

Of course, there is one way that would avoid all the vexing selection problems and make sure that absolutely anyone could be nominated. Several states now have lotteries where everyone can share the joy of the surprised winners. If all the states tossed names chosen at random into hoppers, winners could be narrowed down to a single finalist—For President of the United States, John H. Flugelhorn of the Pepperoni Pizza Parlor of East Westgate, North Dakota! Everybody could be happy with a long-shot and there wouldn't be any front-runner problem or quarrels about delegates.

As for selecting vice-presidential candidates, the best political solution is a multiple vice presidency—say, half a dozen vice presidents.

But since these solutions may not be practical, we'll keep on in the old way, and the Democrats will keep on struggling with their rules.

Delegates who assembled in San Francisco in July 1984 came out better than they had hoped. Before the convention started, Mondale put new life into the campaign with his choice of a running mate. A star was born: GERALDINE FERRARO.

However the campaign developed, the nomination of this congresswoman for vice president seized the imagination of the country and changed American politics.

Speeches by New York Gov. Mario Cuomo, by Jesse Jackson and by the two nominees brought the delegates to their feet. They liked a Mondale who said up front, "Let's tell the truth. Mr. Reagan will raise taxes and so will I. He won't tell you. I just did." The convention ended with waving flags and a rousing medley of George M. Cohan songs, which showed that the Grand Old Party had no monopoly on the Grand Old Flag.

**GREASED POLLS**

*April 1, 1984*

*April 4, 1984*

*April 10, 1984*

**"IT'S LIKE THEY TOLD US AS KIDS—
IF YOU DUG A HOLE DEEP ENOUGH
YOU'D END UP IN CHINA"**

*April 27, 1984*

**"WELL, WHEN YOU WERE DRIVING YOU DENTED THE FENDERS"**
*May 31, 1984*

"I BELIEVE IN FORGIVENESS—I FORGIVE MYSELF—I ALSO FORGIVE
BIGOTRY, HATRED, RACISM, THREATS AND LYING BY ANY OF MY
SUPPORTERS"

*May 4, 1984*

As for the GOP in 1984, it had none of the primary and nomination problems the Democrats did. Since no Republican candidate opposed Reagan, the primary season brought no surprises and no suspense. But the Republican campaign was not really a short one either.

Reagan, who had been running for the presidency for many years, never stopped campaigning—even after he was elected. Almost every one of his free Saturday radio broadcasts was a political speech.

At press conferences, other presidents went directly to questions unless they announced something like major appointments. Reagan began his with political speeches.

Throughout his term, most of the presidential messages were campaign speeches and the trips were campaign trips.

In a remarkable performance, Reagan continued running against the government in Washington—which he had been heading for three and a half years. You would have thought he had just visited the capital city to go slumming.

As for politics stopping at the water's edge—well—it hasn't done that since presidents discovered that trips abroad played well at home. Reagan was the third president to win what one columnist called "The China primary."

There was a new wrinkle in the Reagan trips abroad. Up ahead of the cameramen for the major networks were the cameramen of the Republican National Committee. The timing of foreign meetings and dinners and receptions was jiggered around for live network viewing. But the Reagan campaign filming never fell behind.

An example was the Reagan trip to Korea, where it was announced that he had gone to the front to view North Korea (close-ups of the president as if dressed for combat, looking through field glasses). Later, and farther back, Reagan spoke to the troops from behind a sandbag barricade. Since the enemy was some distance away and the troops themselves seemed to be out in the open, the sandbag lectern hardly seemed necessary. But it made a good picture.

In a sense, Reagan traveled even farther than could be seen on any

"SAY, YOU'RE PRETTY GOOD AT THIS
TOO"

*April 26, 1984*

THE RETURN OF MARATHON
DANCING

*May 18, 1984*

"HE HAS ANSWERS FOR
EVERYTHING"

*December 4, 1983*

"YOU'RE STANDING VERY HIGH IN
THE POLLS"

*January 12, 1984*

*May 15, 1984*

**"IN THE BAD OLD DAYS, THERE USED TO BE POLITICAL MACHINES"**
*March 11, 1984*

**"WE MIGHT HAVE TO ADJUST SOCIAL SECURIGLUB"**
*May 8, 1984*

**"WE'RE TAKING AN EXIT POLL—HOW WOULD YOU LIKE TO MAKE AN EXIT?"**
*December 19, 1980*

WASHINGTON  ADAMS  JEFFERSON  MADISON

200 YEARS SINCE YORKTOWN

©1981 HERBLOCK

*October 21, 1981*

maps. For the 1984 campaign he made departures from previously fixed political positions.

He suddenly seemed to become so interested in the environment that he might have been mistaken for nature boy.

As for negotiations with Russia, he became so flexible that even his knees seemed to bend.

Political campaigns can do remarkable things—while they last.

And now back to the Democrats—running to close gaps in their party and in the polls. In addition to their other 1984 troubles, they had been accused of having an agenda gap.

They had been criticized for having no theme, no new ideas. Well, if there were no bright new ideas, there were still some good old ones —not only to "provide for the common defense," but to "promote the general welfare, and secure the blessings of liberty. . . ."

When Franklin D. Roosevelt first ran for president, he didn't have an outline for what he would do, but he made a simple promise. It was to "return the government of the United States to the people of the United States."

He did, too. ■

**"I'VE BEEN THROUGH LOTS OF
TOUGH SITUATIONS IN THE MOVIES
—WITH GRIT AND A SHOW OF
FORCE, OUR SIDE ALWAYS WINS"**
*July 26, 1983*

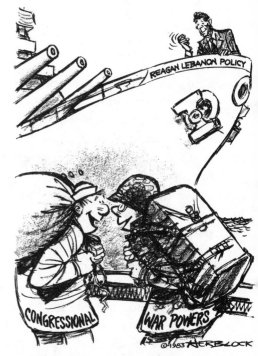

**"GEE, FOR A WHILE THERE, I WAS
AFRAID HE WOULDN'T LET US COME
ALONG"**
*September 21, 1983*

**DELAYED-ACTION BOMBS**
*December 1, 1983*

*December 6, 1983*

# THE
# LITTLE BIG HORN
# LOGBOOK

Everyone is familiar with "The Marines' Hymn," which begins: *From the halls of Montezuma to the shores of Tripoli / We fight our country's battles, in the air, on land, and sea. . . .*

In August 1982, President Reagan dispatched U.S. Marines to the shores of Lebanon, not to "fight our country's battles" but as part of a multinational force (MNF) to supervise the pullout of Palestine Liberation Army troops.

The Marines left Beirut on Sept. 10. But a few days later, after the assassination of Lebanon's president-elect and the massacres at two Palestinian camps, they were returned as part of the MNF to help keep peace. The U.S. Marines took up positions at the Beirut airport.

At the end of 1982, the Marine commander in Lebanon had difficulty in describing to an interviewer the mission of the Marines. "It's rather a unique one of 'presence' not taught at our military schools," he said.

The "presence" became frustrating for the Marines, who found themselves embroiled in a civil war and pinned down in a mission impossible. And a verbal national battle developed at home over the purpose and conduct of the mission.

December 22, 1983

"OUR MILITARY FORCES ARE BACK
ON THEIR FEET AND STANDING
TALL"
—Ronald Reagan
December 13, 1983

"WE'RE FINALLY OVERCOMING THAT
VIETNAM SYNDROME"
December 7, 1983

December 30, 1983

Early in the afternoon of April 18, 1983, a pickup truck loaded with explosives was driven as a "truck bomb" into the front door of the American embassy at Beirut. The explosion killed 17 Americans and 46 Lebanese and destroyed a large part of the embassy building.

On Sept. 8, 1983, U.S. warships stationed offshore began shelling mainland targets in Lebanon.

By October, six more Americans had been killed and 30 more wounded as the Marines themselves became the targets of fire from factional forces. The "peacekeeping" U.S. troops were now in the position of supporting President Amin Gemayel's army in an essentially religious civil war.

Meanwhile back home President Reagan was being questioned about the safety of the mission.

On Oct. 19, 1983, during a White House press conference, three different reporters asked him about the security of the Marines.

> **Q:** Mr. President, there's growing concern about the Marines in Lebanon, and your national security affairs adviser has said that the loss of life is unacceptable and that the partition of Lebanon is unacceptable. What are you going to do about it?
>
> **The President:** Helen [Helen Thomas, United Press International], we're going to keep on doing what we have been doing, trying to complete the plan that we launched a little more than a year ago. We know there are hazards there, and no one can feel more deeply about the loss of life and the wounding of some of our men there. We knew it was a hazardous undertaking when we joined in the multinational force. But our objective remains the same.
>
> We have made great progress there. . . .

Then, after a couple of other questions:

> **Q:** Mr. President, when I was in the Marines the doctrine was to take the high ground and hold it and not deploy on a flat, open field like the Beirut airport. What reason is there to prevent the Marines from taking some more defensible positions in pursuit of the policy for which you've sent them there?
>
> **The President:** Well, Jerry [Jeremiah O'Leary, *Washington Times*], all of those things we're asking ourselves, and we're looking at everything that can be done to try and make their position safer. But you must remember, you were talking about when you were being trained as Marines for combat. And if

**DEJA VU**
*February 8, 1984*

**"LIGHTS—CAMERA—FOG MACHINE—"**
*February 24, 1984*

**"BUT HOW DO WE GET OUT?"**
*January 4, 1984*

*February 10, 1984*

these Marines had gone there to join in the combat on the side of whatever force we might have picked, then all of those rules would apply. But they're there as part of a multinational force to try and maintain a stability. . . .

And a few minutes later, another reporter asked:

**Q:** Mr. President, before the United States went into Vietnam, the French suffered a devastating defeat there by putting their troops in a saucer-shaped depression with the enemy up around the sides shooting down on them. Doesn't this appear uncomfortably similar to you to the way we are deploying our troops in Lebanon on the low ground? And how soon can we expect that we're going to redeploy them to a spot that makes more sense?

**The President:** Well, right now, with the cease-fire, it isn't from high ground that they're being fired upon. Actually, much of this that has tragically taken lives there is literally coming from civilians, from radicals, in residential neighborhoods where we have always refrained from using artillery cover or anything of that kind. And when they were fired upon from the hills, that's when naval gunfire responded, and maybe the French at Dien Bien Phu in that terrible defeat didn't have a New Jersey sitting offshore as we do.

**Q:** But our Marines are still being killed, sir.

**The President:** I know, and, as I say, most of this from the sniper-type fire. . . .

And we're not sitting idly by. We're looking at every option and everything that we can do that can leave us in the position to carry out the mission for which they were sent and, at the same time, make their lives safer.

At dawn on Oct. 23, 1983—four days after the presidential press conference and six months after the truck bombing of the American embassy at Beirut—a truck bomb was driven into a building where 400 Marines were sleeping at the Beirut airport.

The casualties included 241 Americans killed. The building was reduced to rubble. These Marines had been given sleeping quarters in one building because it was thought this would make it easier to protect them.

On Oct. 27, 1983, President Reagan took to the airwaves with an address. He said that the operational mission of the Marines was to secure a piece of Beirut, to keep order in their sector. He said that those who directed the bombing atrocity "must be dealt justice, and

**"NO, THAT ONE IS THE LEBANESE SITUATION—THIS ONE IS THE U.S. ADMINISTRATION'S POLICY EXPLANATIONS"**

*February 15, 1984*

**"NOW THE REASON WE'RE HERE IS TO PROTECT AMERICAN LIVES— OURS"**

*February 17, 1984*

**STANDING TALL**

*February 23, 1984*

**"BOY, WHAT I COULD DO WITH THIS IF SOMEBODY ELSE WAS PRESIDENT"**

*February 28, 1984*

they will be." He said that "we'll do everything we can to insure that our men are as safe as possible" and "We will insure that . . . our Marines are given the greatest possible protection."

All during October 1983, President Reagan asserted that the Marine presence was central to our credibility throughout the world and was vital to help bring peace to Lebanon. It was "key to the region's stability now and in the future."

On Dec. 4, a U.S. Navy jet bombardier-navigator was captured and a pilot was killed when their jet was downed while taking part in U.S. air raids on Syrian anti-aircraft positions.

Late in December 1983, a congressional subcommittee reported on the Lebanon disaster and faulted commanding officers. These findings differed from President Reagan's description of events in his speech of Oct. 27, 1983.

In that speech Mr. Reagan said that the truck "crashed through a series of barriers . . . a chain link fence and barbed wire entanglements. The guards opened fire, but it was too late."

The report said that the driver had only to crash through the fence, and that the Marine sentries did not open fire—their guns were not even loaded.

Also, late in December 1983, a Defense Department commission, headed by retired Adm. Robert L. J. Long, reported *its* findings on the Lebanon disaster to Secretary of Defense Caspar Weinberger. Weinberger delayed the report's public release for a few days so that President Reagan could reply to it before it became public.

On Dec. 27, 1983, President Reagan said that he had soberly considered the commission's word about accountability up and down the chain of command, and "I do not believe . . . that the local commanders on the ground, men who have already suffered quite enough, should be punished for not fully comprehending the nature of today's terrorist threat.

"If there is to be blame, it properly rests here in this office and with this President. And I accept responsibility for the bad as well as the good."

He continued to insist that "the presence of the multinational force has made some progress. . . ."

The commander-in-chief's "I accept responsibility" statement

**"ON TO CENTRAL AMERICA!"**
*March 13, 1984*

came two months after the disaster and *only* after two commissions delivered severe reports. It was a gesture that simply eliminated the possibility of anyone being disciplined and, in effect, kicked under the rug the responsibility of everyone—including Reagan.

On the next day, Dec. 28, 1983, the Defense Department released the Long Commission report. It held commanders responsible for their subordinates and stated that "the responsibility of military commanders is absolute." The report criticized a policy that places military efforts over diplomacy. It said there was an "urgent need" for a reassessment of the Marines' role in Lebanon, "where initial conditions had dramatically changed."

In contrast to Reagan's repeated reports of "progress," the commission concluded that U.S. policy in Lebanon "over the past 15 months" had been, "to a large degree, characterized by an emphasis on military options and the expansion of the U.S. military role"—an "expansion of our military involvement" that "greatly increased the risk to our forces."

In his statement on the Long report, Reagan discussed terrorism as a new and difficult phenomenon. But terrorism had been on the minds of the public and politicians even before the Iranian hostage crisis of 1979–81, which candidate Reagan had found to be a shameful example of our government's weakness.

Within the first week of the Reagan administration in 1981, Secretary of State Alexander Haig stated that terrorism was the administration's number one concern in foreign policy, and President Reagan had said that we would deal with terrorism effectively.

The Long Commission pointed out that the Marines in Lebanon were "not trained, organized, staffed, or supported to deal with the terrorist threat."

It also found that the environment for the Marines had become more hostile and significantly worse after U.S. warships, intervening on behalf of the Lebanese army, shelled Moslem militia positions.

Members of Congress had long been critical of a Lebanon policy that changed from one involving supervision of troop withdrawal, to "peacekeeping," to active participation in a civil war, and one in which the Marines were a "presence"—and vulnerable to attack. A woman whose son was killed—gunned down in Beirut as he was landing in a helicopter—said, "I blame the whole system for letting that happen. There was no protection, no cover. What else could you call them but sitting ducks?"

One of the most telling statements was made by Rep. Sam M. Gibbons (D-Fla.). He said, "If we are there to keep the peace, then we are far too few. If we are there to fight, then we are far too few. If we are there to die, then we are far too many."

As more and more members of both political parties urged an end to the Marine involvement in Lebanon, President Reagan insisted that those who advocated withdrawal wanted to "bug out," and said he would not cut and run.

**"IT'S ALL THE FAULT OF PEOPLE WHO SAID
I WAS MAKING A MISTAKE"**

*April 6, 1984*

In an interview on Feb. 2, 1984, he said about Speaker of the House Tip O'Neill that "He may be ready to surrender, but I'm not." This was the Tip O'Neill who in September 1983 had given Reagan wide latitude by keeping congressional colleagues in line to vote for an 18-month Marine presence in Lebanon. The swipe at O'Neill came at a time when President Reagan had already set in motion the plans for withdrawing the Marines to ships—an action he called "redeployment." This was precisely the withdrawal that O'Neill and many other congressmen had recently been urging.

On Feb. 25, 1984, the American flag that flew over the Marine position was lowered. The American casualties now numbered 280 dead and 168 wounded.

After the accusations about bugging out, Reagan left his announcement of the withdrawal to be made by subordinates, while he, too, withdrew—to California. Like a sun dial, he showed only the brightest hours—and those often with the aid of artificial light.

While the Marines withdrew, the 16-inch guns of the battleship New Jersey fired away as if they were proclaiming a triumph.

When the de-mothballed New Jersey was on its way to Lebanon, Reagan had asked a group of editors, "Did you ever hear a 16-inch gun go off?" Around Beirut they were heard, but they didn't bring the desired result.

Taking battleships out of mothballs might not have been so bad if there had not also come out of mothballs with them the idea that the appearance of these warships would have people in other parts of the world crying, "Big iron dragon in water! Make great thunder and fire!"

As the 16-inch guns blasted at distant hills, military personnel said that the sound was deafening, although they had no idea what they were hitting. But the guns thundering away were a nice dramatic touch. They made the withdrawal seem less like a retreat, even if only to people over here who read about the guns or saw them on television.

As the Marines departed, their headquarters position was taken over, not by President Gemayel's army, which they had supported, but by waiting Moslem militiamen.

Reagan continued to insist that there had been no failure in Lebanon, but he no longer assigned that country a key role, saying now that "Lebanon's troubles are just part of the overall problem in the Middle East."

On March 30, 1984, the warships off Lebanon quietly departed with most of the Marines aboard.

Less than a week later, when the question of Lebanon and blame were raised at a news conference, President Reagan said that Congress "must take a responsibility." He went on:

> When you're engaged in this kind of a diplomatic attempt and you have forces there, and there is an effort made to oust them, a debate as public as was conducted here, raging with the Congress demanding, Oh, bring our men home, take them away. All this can do is stimulate the terrorists and urge them on to further attacks because they see a possibility of success in getting the force out, which is keeping them from having their way. And it should be understood by everyone in government that once this is committed, you have rendered them ineffective when you conduct that kind of a debate in public.

So the blame did not rest with the Joint Chiefs of Staff, who had warned against the original dispatch of Marines to Beirut. The blame did not sit on the doorsteps of anyone in the chain of command, because Reagan had cleared them in his I-accept-responsibility statement. The blame did not lie with the commander-in-chief or with his policies or with the changing purposes of the mission. The blame was with Congress! *Congress and public debate!* Congress and criticism —the same criticism that Ronald Reagan had so long directed at other presidents.

One high administration official suggested that when congressmen disagreed with the president on foreign policy, they might better express their views in letters to the White House rather than in public speeches.

That's what was wrong—our constitutional form of government with its co-equal branches—that and public debate, the kind of thing that goes on in democracies.

Our patriotic leaders speak emotionally about our wonderful free country and God bless America. Ah, but if only they could run it a little more like our wicked enemies run *their* countries!  ∎

# REPAIRS AND SERVICE

On an out-of-town trip, I checked into a hotel just in time to catch a television program I was anxious to see. But the TV set in my room was not working, and no amount of frantic fiddling with the knobs produced anything. I phoned the desk and told them about it, and they said their TV repairman would be up soon. Sure enough, in a short time there was a knock at the door by a man who announced himself as "Repair." He went to the TV, looked it over, and then gave the side of the set a whop with his hand. Instantly it came to life and from then on all channels functioned beautifully.

This made me nostalgic, not just for the early days of television but for a time when things could be fixed without every repair job turning out to be a Great Big Deal.

Attempts to correct malfunctions of government sometimes employ the use of a baseball bat, an ax, and a set of tools used for complete disassembly. When Ronald Reagan ran for president, he sounded as if the whole U.S. government ought to be recalled.

We've all heard about sins of commission and omission. What candidate Reagan talked about were sins of commissions—horrible examples of regulations that were said to be strangling business and

**"I WAS JUST—UH—DEMONSTRATING
A TYPE OF PASSIVE RESTRAINT"**
*June 18, 1982*

**"SAVE THE CAR!"**
*April 8, 1981*

**"ALL WE'RE DOING NOW IS TAKING A
LOOK"**
*August 18, 1981*

**"THANKS, PAL—NOW IS THERE ANY
WAY YOU CAN KEEP THOSE TRICKY
JAPANESE AUTO MAKERS FROM
INSTALLING THEM IN *THEIR* CARS?"**
*November 3, 1981*

stifling the economy. When he became president, consumers began learning about sins of omission. Reagan appointees who were non-believers in public protection gave us many omissions of enforcement in the agencies they took over.

One of these agencies is the National Highway Traffic Safety Administration (NHTSA), which is supposed to advance the kind of thing its name implies.

In 1977, during the Carter administration, and after years of study, the NHTSA issued a regulation to introduce into American cars "passive restraints"—air bags or automatic seat belts that did not require buckling. It was estimated that these would annually save 12,000 lives and prevent 100,000 serious injuries. The regulation did not call for unreasonably quick compliance. It gave years of lead time for the auto industry to begin installing these safety devices.

In 1981, Mr. Reagan's appointees to the NHTSA decided to restrain the restraints. They threw out the requirement for automatic safety devices.

But that didn't end the matter. In 1983, the U.S. Supreme Court ruled that the current appointees to the NHTSA had exceeded their authority by arbitrarily scrapping that agency's previous work. The "passive restraint" issue was sent back for further study.

On July 11, 1984, the Department of Transportation announced an airbag decision that might have been prepared by windbags. It provided for the restraints in the future—unless a certain number of states made seat belt use mandatory, etc. etc. etc. It gave the administration a position in favor of airbags, but with holes in it. And it made car manufacturers happy. Meanwhile, thousands of lives would continue to be lost.

During this same year the NHTSA also decided to scrap another requirement—standards for automobile tire treadwear to give the motorist better protection at the tire shop and on the road. This time the U.S. Court of Appeals slapped down the NHTSA, which it said was "arbitrary and capricious" in junking the tire standards.

In another case before the courts, consumer groups were trying to force the NHTSA to require stronger automobile bumpers. It hardly seems too much to ask that a bumper withstand bumps at five miles an hour instead of 2½ miles an hour.

**"MIGHT AS WELL TURN IT OFF—
AFTER ALL, THERE'S NO OIL IN IT"**
*February 5, 1982*

**"WE'RE SHREWDLY BURNING OUR
BRIDGES *BEFORE* US"**
*June 7, 1981*

**"HURRY—WE'VE STRUCK OIL!"**
*January 15, 1984*

**"SMOOTH"**
*April 28, 1982*

In addition to the automobile safety cases, the courts overturned other actions by Reagan administration agencies. One had weakened protections against the pollution of water. Another had weakened protections against exposure of workers to dangerous chemicals.

The Supreme Court had to step in again to require administration appointees to enforce the Occupational Safety and Health Act. The Court did this in a ruling to protect workers from such hazardous substances as cotton dust.

The Federal Trade Commission (FTC) was another regulatory agency to which Reagan appointed non-regulators. Nevertheless in 1984, some of the FTC members' previous years of efforts finally paid off. Rules were established requiring the funeral industry to quote prices and actual options to the bereaved. Such people had long been easy prey for undertakers to whom the customer's pocketbook was the real "loved one."

The Environmental Protection Agency was, in effect, "deregulated" by the Reagan administration, which appointed overseers who seemed happy in the environment of pollution industry lobbyists. The Interior Department was turned over to people whose sympathies were with private "developers" rather than with public conservationists.

In its eagerness to deregulate, to get the government out of governing and to turn things over to business, the administration proposed selling to private interests the satellites of the National Weather Service. But the prospect of a highly publicized yard sale of those national properties proved unpopular. Both houses of Congress voted a resolution that registered "no sale."

The Energy Department, which Reagan had originally scheduled for demolition, survived in a listless way. It showed little energy for encouraging conservation or for developing new sources of power.

Deregulation of the oil industry, begun under President Carter, was speeded up under President Reagan. Whatever this deregulation accomplished, it did not result in large new findings of oil down in the ground. The big action has been coming in high-finance offices, where owners of giant oil companies discovered oil in the tanks of smaller competitors that they took over. These acquisitions added

January 3, 1982

**"NOW THE BIG ONES ARE EATING
THE BIG ONES"**

March 16, 1984

**"YOU WANT TO BORROW A FEW
THOUSAND DOLLARS TO BUY STOCK?
WE CAN'T LEND MONEY FOR THAT
PURPOSE"**

October 7, 1982

**"IT LOOKS OKAY FROM UP HERE"**

December 15, 1982

"ORVILLE, I FORESEE OVERCROWDED AIRPORTS, LOST
LUGGAGE, ENDLESS HOLDING PATTERNS, DISPUTES OVER SALES OF
WARPLANES, STRIKES BY AIR CONTROLLERS—TO HELL WITH IT"

*August 12, 1981*

**"FREE! FREE! FREE!"**
*September 30, 1983*

**"WE'RE EXPERIENCING A LITTLE
TEMPORARY TURBULENCE"**
*November 23, 1983*

**"MR WATSON, OR SOMEBODY—COME
HERE, I WANT YOU"**
*November 13, 1983*

**SORCERER'S APPRENTICE**
*November 25, 1983*

nothing to the nation's oil supply but subtracted some service stations affiliated with the companies that were gobbled up.

Airline deregulation was also carried forward from the previous administration, and with mixed results. Some routes gained increased competition; some lost what service they had; some fares went down and others went up. This left many consumers up in the air. Many more were left in holding patterns on the ground because of delayed flights at overcrowded airports.

Still another example of deregulation begun under Jimmy Carter affected the trucking industry. This was never popular with the Teamsters union, which supported Reagan. And under his administration, further deregulation came to a halt.

With the approval of Congress, state controls over trucking were run over. Truckers got the green light to send wider and longer double-trailer trucks into every state of the union—including those that had previously protected their citizens and their roads from these double-trouble behemoths. The cost of additional road repairs alone will be great, and the cost in public safety greater.

In 1983, there occurred a form of deregulation that grabbed the country by the ears. An anti-trust case against the Bell Telephone Co. was carried to what phone subscribers considered its illogical conclusion.

A system that could have continued working well with just an occasional whop on the side was dismantled and parts left spread all over the country. This brought chaos out of order. Rates went up, service went down, and confusion reigned supreme. Phone users heard the voices of many phone companies—with many new charges and rates. And the screams of subscribers could be heard across the entire country without the aid of any telephone equipment at all.

The nation's oldest communication system was given a complete overhaul in 1970. That was when the government gave up control of the Post Office Department, headed by a postmaster general in the Cabinet, and set up an independent government-owned corporation —the U.S. Postal (here-comes-the-funny-part) *Service.* This semi-autonomous organization combines private monopoly with federal bureaucracy, retaining the worst features of both. Even early con-

**"THIS LOOKS LIKE A PERSONAL LETTER—WHY DON'T YOU USE THE PHONE?"**

*June 24, 1983*

**"NO, THAT'S THE PRICE—THE SERVICE IS DOWN HERE"**

*November 4, 1983*

**"IT'S A HELL OF A WAY TO RUN A 'SERVICE' "**

*June 24, 1981*

**"WE ALWAYS RING TWICE"**

*July 23, 1981*

gressional sponsors of this "service" concede now that it was a mistake.

Postal officials keep telling us that we have the best postal system in the world, and hope that repetition will make the claim believable. But these statements do not impress anyone who waits three days or more for first-class mail to get across town—or a week or so for letters to travel between Washington and New York or Baltimore.

Postal Service officials have long maintained that each type of mail pays only for itself. Not so.

In February 1984, the Federal Trade Commission charged the Postal Service with using revenues from first-class mail to subsidize its "E-Com Service"—an electronic-and-postal combination for businesses. E-Com lost millions of dollars a year. It was one of the greatest losers since the package-sorting-machinery fiasco, in which the Postal Service dropped $1 billion on equipment and a system that didn't work.

The Postal Service spends money to advertise how good it is. But television commercial spots are expensive; and every time we see that postal eagle flapping across our TV screens it's costing us. And, indirectly, so are the TV commercials in which the well-heeled postal unions, paid by the Postal Service, tell us what a wonderful job *they* are doing.

The TV eagle is not the postal department's only high flier. For his travels around the country, Postmaster General William F. Bolger in 1982 leased a jet plane for $47,000 a month. He later had the Postal Service buy the plane, at a cost of $1.65 million.

We could buy a lot of first-class stamps for that money, and we did—with no better first-class service. The same day Bolger announced his leasing arrangement to the postal board of governors, they were applying for a $3.5 billion rate increase.

Reporting on this story in the *Federal Times,* Bob Williams noted that the Federal Aviation Agency maintains at least four executive jets at nearby National Airport—and he cited a newspaper report that between November 1983 and February 1984, half of the special Postal Service plane's flights carried only one passenger.

Somebody was getting prompt first-class service: the postmaster general.

**"I FEEL SICK"**

*July 26, 1981*

**"AND TO THE SURPRISE OF NO ONE
—THE WINNER!"**

*August 4, 1981*

**"DID YOU HEAR TALK ABOUT
PUTTING A CAP ON THE TAX CUT?"**

*June 29, 1983*

**"WHAT—SPEND SOME TIME IN THAT
DUMP RUBBING ELBOWS WITH THE
COMMON PEOPLE?"**

*January 9, 1983*

In the fall of 1983, the Postal Service predicted a whopping deficit for 1984–85 and asked for a first-class rate increase of 3 cents. But by the summer of 1984, it turned out that instead of a deficit, there would likely be a small surplus. Nevertheless, the postmaster general continued to press for a 23-cent stamp.

If presidents don't want the responsibility of bringing the postal department back into the government, an administration interested in increasing private enterprise could at least foster some competition in the letter delivery department. The time has come for first-class service to be returned to first-class mail.

A long-time candidate for a major overhaul is the federal tax structure. Thorough reform would need an awful lot of cooperation between the White House and Congress. It would probably have to involve a suspension of rules, a suspension of politics and a suspension of disbelief.

The Social Security system always seems to need some kind of repair, even after we've been assured that the latest improvement should last a while. With the aid of a presidential bipartisan commission, Congress did a repair job on it in 1983. One reform brought future federal employees into the system—a provision fought tooth and nail by government employee unions. Sen. Robert Dole (R-Kan.), chairman of the Senate Finance Committee, scored a win on this one but a loss on another reform. That one was designed to mend a costly hole in tax collections by having banks withhold a portion of interest and dividend payments to cover taxes. Federal losses due to unreported income in these categories was estimated at $5 billion a year.

This law, similar to the withholding of taxes due on salaries, would not have affected people in lower-income brackets. But the banking lobby roused small depositors with the idea that this was a new tax on them. The bankers created an unprecedented blizzard of mail, which left Congress with frozen feet. They repealed the reform before it ever took effect.

When you get into overhauls, the full-scale jobs are constitutional amendments. My top priority is an amendment providing for voting representation in Congress for the District of Columbia. As of 1984

**BANK WITHHOLDUP**
*April 22, 1983*

*May 20, 1983*

**"THEY SEEM TO BE GETTING
FARTHER AWAY FROM US"**
*January 17, 1982*

**"THAT'S A HEFTY BILL TO PAY, BUT
IT'S WORTH IT TO KNOW THEY
FINALLY GOT THE CAR IN GOOD
SHAPE"**
*June 26, 1980*

**PUMPING CARDBOARD**
*July 13, 1982*

**"LOOK—MY WIFE IS A WOMAN, MY MOTHER WAS A WOMAN, BOTH OF MY DAUGHTERS ARE WOMEN . . ."**
*July 17, 1983*

**"BUT HARK!"**
*January 18, 1983*

**"YOU HAD A VERY PROFITABLE YEAR. LET'S SEE—AFTER SPECIAL TAX BREAKS AND SUBSIDIES, WE OWE YOU . . ."**
*November 27, 1981*

**"PROPOSED U.S. CONSTITUTIONAL AMENDMENT NUMBER 98—TO ELIMINATE WASTE, WANT, LUST, RINGWORM, AND RUDE BEHAVIOR . . . "**

*July 14, 1981*

this was the only constitutional amendment passed by Congress and making the rounds of the states.

The people of the District—sometimes called the Last Colony—serve in the armed forces and are subject to all the laws of the United States. They pay local taxes, including a District income tax, and all federal taxes, including the federal income tax. They really have taxation without representation.

The Equal Rights Amendment deserves another try in Congress and the nation. But the right to elect voting representatives to Congress is absolutely basic. The women—and men—who live in the District of Columbia don't even have that.

There have been proposals for all kinds of other amendments, and in most cases I think Congress could skip them.

One proposed amendment would require a federal balanced budget—although it's hard to see how such an amendment could avoid loopholes, even if it were desirable. But the push for this amendment has made progress through almost enough state legislatures to bring about a call for a constitutional convention.

Up to now, we've had only one constitutional convention, and I don't think a second one would improve on the job done by Washington, Jefferson, Madison, Adams and company.

If such a convention would open up the whole constitution, I don't even want to hear an estimate on it. I don't want that kind of overhaul at all. Except to repair a couple of inequities, the constitution is in good condition. If a constitutional convention wants to tinker with it, I'm ready to go down to the National Archives Building, stand in front of that document and tell them "You ain't taking it back to the shop." ∎

# Final Note

"HA, HA, IT'S JUST A JOKE—THIS ONE'S NOT EVEN CONNECTED"

*August 14, 1984*